W9-CDJ-450

A RABBI LOOKS AT THE

AFTERLIFE

A RABBI LOOKS AT THE
AFTERLIFE

A NEW LOOK AT HEAVEN AND HELL
WITH STORIES OF PEOPLE WHO'VE BEEN THERE

JONATHAN BERNIS

DESTINY IMAGE® PUBLISHERS, INC.

P.O. Box 310, Shippensburg, PA 17257-0310

"Promoting Inspired Lives."

This book and all other Destiny Image and Destiny Image Fiction books are available at Christian bookstores and distributors worldwide.

For more information on foreign distributors, call 717-532-3040.

Reach us on the Internet: www.destinyimage.com.

ISBN 13: HC 978-0-7684-0745-7

ISBN 13: TP 978-0-7684-0410-4

ISBN 13 EBook: 978-0-7684-0411-1

For Worldwide Distribution, Printed in the U.S.A.

1 2 3 4 5 6 7 8 / 18 17 16 15 14

CONTENTS

Part One

INTRODUCTION

Chapter 1

IS THERE LIFE AFTER DEATH?

WHERE WILL YOU GO when you die?

Will you find yourself in paradise, surrounded by love, joy, and peace?

Or will you pass from life into a place of torment, regret, and never-ending sorrow?

Some say you'll simply cease to exist, returning to the nothingness you knew—or rather, didn't know—before you were even born.

There is no more important question to ask than, "What will happen to me when I die?"

After all, no matter how young or healthy you may be, you're going to die someday. We all will. And no matter how many years a person might live, it is a very short time compared to eternity. Obviously, we should all do everything we possibly can to prepare for what lies ahead. If there is something we can do to ensure a happy afterlife, then by all means, we ought to do it!

Will Rogers once said that the only two things certain in life are death and taxes. If you know all the loopholes and have a smart attorney, you may get out of paying taxes. But nobody—and I do mean nobody—can cheat death.

Death is inescapable. One of my favorite comic writers is Woody Allen. He is obsessed with death and dying and turns his insecurity into an art form with his on-screen characters. He was once quoted as saying, "I don't want to achieve immortality through my work. I want to achieve it through not dying."

Sorry, Woody. That's not going to happen. Every human being who has ever lived before us has died, with two possible exceptions according to the Bible—Enoch (Genesis 5:24) and Elijah (2 Kings 2:11). Based on what we've seen so far, we can pretty much assume that death is going to come for each of us.

A few years ago, the U.S. government spent billions of dollars to bail out several big banks and two of the big three automakers. The rationale for this huge expense was that these businesses were "too big to fail." In other words, the feeling was that their failure would have such a huge negative impact on the American economy that it just couldn't be allowed. And yet, no human being is "too big to die." Kings and presidents die. Brilliant physicists and philosophers die. Beautiful actresses and rock stars die. Super-human athletes and great leaders die. Everyone dies. Death is the great equalizer. Rich, poor, black, white, male, female, tall, short, beautiful, ugly—everyone is equal in the grave.

I'm sure you've been touched by death in one way or another. We all have. Most of us have lost parents, friends, or other loved ones. We may wonder where they are. Are they happy? Do they have an awareness of what's going on in our lives? Are they proud of us when we succeed; do they weep with us in our moments of sorrow and loss?

We are also aware of political leaders, sports heroes, and celebrities who have died. They may have been people we looked up to and admired. Elvis Presley and John Lennon are dead. So are Marilyn Monroe, Nelson Mandela, John F. Kennedy, and Ronald Reagan. They seemed bigger than life. Then they were gone. Again, nobody is exempt. We are all going to die.

And after death…where do we go?

WHY I'M WRITING THIS BOOK

My purpose in writing this book is to try to fill in the blanks by exploring what the Bible, both Old and New Testaments, has to say on the subject. We'll explore the ancient Jewish concepts of heaven and hell and look at what Jews believe today. How does this differ from the historic Christian view? And finally, I will share the experiences of six (out of more than a dozen) people I interviewed over a one-year period from all different backgrounds who claimed to have traveled beyond the veil and visited heaven or hell.

Most of the six billion people in the world today believe that life continues after death. Human beings have always had an intuitive feeling that there must be something more than this life.

As Dinesh D'Souza writes in his book *Life After Death:*

> Across the cultures of the world, both East and West,
> and right through the long march of history, people
> have affirmed that this life is one chapter in a larger

story of existence, and that there is life after death…. Many of the world's greatest scientists and philosophers…From John Locke to Isaac Newton…affirmed their belief in the afterlife. Even skeptical Enlightenment figures such as Thomas Paine, Thomas Jefferson, and Benjamin Franklin professed similar views. Europe is the only continent where a bare majority of people believe in the afterlife. By contrast nearly 80 percent of Americans today affirm life after death, and the percentage is even higher, in fact close to 100 percent, in non-Western cultures.[1]

Most of us continue to believe in life after death despite many scientists' attempts to convince us that we are nothing more than the evolution of slime over millions of years. Their belief has been that everything we do, say, and think is controlled by our brains. When our brains die, they say, everything that makes us who we are dies with them.

But most of us know instinctively that this is not the case. If we are merely machines controlled by our brains, then where did our emotions come from? How did we learn to love our parents, our spouses, our children, and our friends? How did we come to understand the difference between right and wrong, and why do we get a guilty conscience when we do something we know we shouldn't do? Who or what told us we shouldn't do it?

In his classic *Mere Christianity*, C.S. Lewis writes about what he calls "The Law of Human Nature" or "The Moral Law." He says:

> Whenever you find a man who says he does not believe
> in real Right and Wrong, you will find the same man

going back on this a moment later. He may break his promise to you, but if you try breaking one to him he will complain "It's not fair," before you can say Jack Robinson. A nation may say treaties do not matter; but then, next minute, they spoil their case by saying the particular treaty they want to break is an unfair one.... It seems then, we are forced to believe in a real Right and Wrong.[2]

Lewis is making an extremely strong case for the existence of a grand design—and a Grand Designer—behind the universe. As he points out, all of the world's various cultures see right and wrong in much the same way:

Think of a country where men were admired for running away in battle, or where a man felt proud of double-crossing all the people who had been kindest to him. You might just as well try to imagine a country where two and two made five.... Selfishness has never been admired. Men have differed as to whether you ought to have one wife or four. But they have always agreed that you must not simply have any woman you liked.[3]

Lewis also presents a compelling argument against those who say that humans engage in "right" behavior because of ingrained instinct:

If two instincts are in conflict, and there is nothing in a creature's mind except those two instincts, obviously the stronger of the two must win. But at those moments when we are most conscious of the Moral Law, it seems to be telling us to side with the weaker of the two impulses. You probably want to be safe, much more than you want to help the man who is drowning; but the Moral Law tells you to help him all the same.… The Moral Law is not any one instinct or any set of instincts: it is something which makes a kind of tune (the tune which we call goodness or right conduct) by directing the instincts.[4]

This is where I personally have one of my biggest philosophical problems with the theory of evolution. It's one thing to believe that, over billions of years, our bodies evolved from tiny one-celled organisms into human beings, with trillions of cells doing highly specialized tasks. Frankly, it boggles the mind to think that this could happen by chance, without a master plan or a creative force behind it. As well, evolution fails to explain how life could form from non-life. But what is perhaps most difficult for me to imagine is that one day the switch suddenly turned on and living creatures began to think. Physical changes are one thing, the ability to think and reason is an entirely other matter.

René Descartes called this "dualism." He famously said, "I think, therefore I am." In other words, we do more than observe and accept the things we see at face value. We analyze. We probe. We are even capable of doubting what we see and of exercising free will.

Philosopher John Locke, in Book IV of the *Essay*, imagines what would happen if, one night while they were sleeping, a prince and a cobbler suddenly exchanged consciousness. When they woke up the next morning, would they be the men they were when they first went to sleep? The answer is yes, they would have the same bodies they had before. But would they be the same person? No—because each would now have the memories and consciousness of the other. Personal identity, Locke argues, is not the same as having the same physical substance. There is something more that makes us who we truly are.

Dinesh D'Souza writes:

> Without free will, even collective decisions become involuntary. If there is no free will, the American founders didn't choose to adopt a Constitution in Philadelphia. Nor did Americans elect Barack Obama president. Nor is there anything we can decide to do to improve Social Security or Medicare. If free will is an illusion, then there are no good deeds or bad deeds because no one has any choice in the matter.[5]

D'Souza points to Immanuel Kant, who argued in his book *Religion within the Limits of Reason Alone,* that morality is an indispensable part of being human. D'Souza writes:

> No human culture has existed without morality. In fact, no normal human being can altogether reject morality; people who are unable to distinguish right from wrong are considered psychopaths. Treat any materialist with inhumane brutality—not as a person, but as an object—and he will indignantly protest, "You shouldn't have done that!" Try as he might, the materialist cannot completely get away from morality. Morality is an incontrovertible fact in the world no less real than any other fact.[6]

D'Souza continues:

We have now found two central features of human nature—consciousness and free will—that are irreducible to matter and appear to be independent from it. Even more remarkable, consciousness and free will have no natural explanation and seem to function beyond the bounds of physical law. Things that are defined by physical law, such as human bodies and human brains, are perishable or destructible. Consciousness and free will, unbound by those constraints, are not. Moreover, consciousness and free will are the defining features of the human soul, which requires awareness, and choices in order to discriminate between right and wrong. The implication is that whatever happens to our bodies and brains after death, our souls live on.[7]

POLITICALLY INCORRECT?

While belief in life after death is positive and I believe part of the "divine programing" instilled in all humans, I am concerned by the growing perception that death is followed by eternal paradise, no matter what we may have believed or how we have behaved in this life. This and the idea that "all roads lead to the same destination" is a dangerous conviction. I fear for the thousands of people who pass into eternity every day, completely unprepared for what may lie ahead.

Yes, I am convinced that life continues beyond the grave. I'll share my many reasons for this as we continue on our search for understanding together. But I certainly do not believe that there are many paths to God, or that any religion will get you to heaven if you practice it sincerely. It may be politically correct to say, "Your religion is just as good as mine," or "What you believe is true for you and what I believe is true for me." But we're not after political correctness here. We're after truth.

My goal in writing this book is to help you find the truth as revealed in the Bible. I believe the Bible is our textbook for life… and death. The Scriptures (both the Old and New Testaments) reveal what exists beyond this life and what we must believe and do to arrive at the proper destination.

And the truth, according to what the Bible teaches, is that there is a very narrow road that leads to heaven. But more on that later.

IS TRUTH ABSOLUTE?

One of my favorite writers, the late theologian and philosopher Francis Schaeffer, had quite a bit to say about the importance of "True Truth," or absolute truth, versus "subjective truth," the notion that truth changes depending on the perspective and situation.

In powerful works like *The God Who Is There, Escape from Reason, How Shall We Then Live,* and *Whatever Happened to the Human Race?,* Schaeffer showed clearly the negative impact that comes from rejecting the absolutes of God's Word.

"If there are no absolutes by which to judge society, then society is absolute," Schaeffer wrote.[8]

And if society is absolute, then whatever society deems as proper *is* proper. As an example, let's take the case of Nazi Germany. The Nazis believed and taught that is was necessary to rid the world of the Jews and the mentally and physically ill in order to build an Aryan super race. Did this belief make it true or right? Of course not! Yet no end of atrocities is possible if we say there is no such thing as absolute truth. I know this is an extreme example, but it is a harsh illustration of where subjective truth can lead in a world void of absolutes.

Schaeffer once said that in our age, the only absolute allowed is the absolute insistence that there is no absolute.

Schaeffer died 30 years ago, and I believe what he predicted has already come to pass. Today, one of the biggest faux pas anyone can commit is to appear to be intolerant of another's point of view. If I say the Muslim religion is intolerant of the infidel or that the Koran teaches hate, then I'm considered to be a bigot. If someone believes he can get to heaven by dancing naked in his garden every night at midnight, I'm supposed to smile and say, "Well, everyone has their own truth." If I believe in the existence of hell, then I'm being narrow and judgmental.

But what if something really is true? Does my denial of that fact make it any less so? I may reject the truth that there is an unseen force called gravity, but if I jump out the window of a ten story building I will fall to my death...regardless what I believed would or would not happen.

In our case, if the Bible tells us that hell exists, but I say it doesn't, does my "truth" have equal value with biblical truth? If we both see a red truck being driven down the street but I tell you, "There goes a blue truck," does that make it any less red?

Francis Schaeffer believed that the loss of the concept of absolute truth had caused Westerners to abandon reason. This in turn has led to an increasing fascination with existential philosophy, drugs, and Eastern religion. Schaeffer believed, as I have also come to believe, that the Bible provides us with absolute truth, and the standard by which all else must be measured. We may not like some of the things we read in the book, but that won't make them any less so. Like you, I'm not at all comfortable with the concept of hell. I don't want to think of anyone suffering for eternity. But there is absolutely nothing I can do to make it any less true.

WHY THIS BOOK IS UNIQUE

What makes this book different from other books on this subject? Several things.

1. As a *Messianic rabbi*, I have a perspective on Judaism and Christianity, as well as the Scriptures, that differs from those raised in one faith or the other. I have involvement in both. So this book looks at both religions' view of the afterlife historically, as well as digs into the nuances between the two testaments on this important topic.

Let me take a moment to explain what I mean when I refer to myself as a Messianic rabbi. As I explained in my book *A Rabbi Looks at Jesus of Nazareth,* if you're Jewish and you ask your rabbi about me, he or she will probably tell you that I am not a rabbi. Why? Because "rabbi," in the Jewish world, indicates someone who has studied at a recognized Jewish institution and has been ordained by a mainstream, recognized Jewish body.

Although I do not meet this particular criteria, I am ordained, and have served in ministry for more than 30 years. I am also credentialed by one of two recognized national Messianic Jewish organizations and have an extensive background in theology that would meet the educational criteria of a Jewish rabbi.

2. As the host of the television program *Jewish Voice with Jonathan Bernis,* I researched and personally interviewed at least a dozen people who claim to have had glimpses of the afterlife. They

are among more than 18 million Americans who have had Near-Death Experiences (NDEs). Every one of the people I interviewed had a fascinating story to tell. Without exception, their lives were changed forever by what they experienced. I will share six of the most compelling stories with you.

3. *As a Jewish believer in Jesus,* I have spent the past 34 years of my life sharing with people my personal experiences and what I have learned about the reality of God and the afterlife. I was a college student when I had a supernatural encounter that completely transformed my life. This experience and what I learned in the months that followed changed my goals for the future, my purpose in life, my desires, my relationships with my friends and family—literally everything, including and most importantly my worldview. As a Jew who has come to accept both that the Bible is true and that Jesus (Yeshua) is the Jewish Messiah foretold in the Torah and prophets, I have a unique perspective on this topic.

Both the Old and New Testaments have a great deal to say about what happens to the soul after death. Together we'll take a very close look at these Scriptures. We'll also explore the Mishnah and other sections of the Talmud. We'll discuss the mysticism of the Kabbalah. And, as I mentioned earlier, we'll even take a brief look at what different cultures and religions have to say about life after death, and consider what some ancient civilizations have believed.

But not everything can be learned through the study of ancient civilizations or scholarly books, even if one of those books is the Bible. In the end, this is a faith proposition. I believe that when presented with all the evidence, the conclusions are clear.

My challenge to you as you read: *decide what you believe and act on it in this life to determine your eternity.* Please consider what you read carefully, with an open heart and mind. Your eternity may be hanging in the balance.

Chapter 2

HEAVEN, HELL, AND NEAR-DEATH EXPERIENCES

It's not very popular to believe in hell these days. The very idea seems like a relic from a barbaric age. A reminder of the days when the Roman Catholic Church sold indulgences, which were basically insurance policies guaranteeing that the holder would not go to hell.

Actually, indulgences were sold to help souls gain an early release from purgatory, where, according to the Roman Catholic Church, they were being purified through pain to be made fit for heaven. These indulgences were often sold at very high prices to impoverished people who could not afford them.

The problem with purgatory and such teachings is that they are not to be found anywhere in the Bible, neither Old Testament nor New. In fact, it was this corrupt practice of selling indulgences, more than anything else, that inspired Martin Luther to nail his 95

Theses to the door of Castle Church in Wittenberg, Germany, and thereby launch the Protestant Reformation.

As mentioned previously, the prevailing attitude today, especially in the Western world, seems to be that death offers a new beginning to everyone, no matter how they've lived or what they believed. According to this thinking, when you die you'll be greeted and welcomed by your loved ones who've already reached the other side. All your sins are immediately forgiven. Everything is light, love, peace, and beauty. If there is a God and He is a God of love, then heaven is a wonderful place where all of *God's children* go after they die. And if God is all loving, then He would not leave anyone out. Everyone will be there. If so many people in the world believe so many different things, all paths must lead to the same God and the same heaven. Sounds great, doesn't it?

Best-selling author N.T. Wright, Bishop of Durham for the Church of England, writes, "After [Princess] Diana's death one message left in London spoke as in the princess's own voice: 'I did not leave you at all. I am still with you. I am in the sun and in the wind. I am even in the rain. I did not die, I am with you all.' Many funerals, memorial services, and even funerary inscriptions now give voice to this kind of belief. Many would-be Christians try to persuade themselves and others that this kind of ongoing life is really what is meant by traditional teaching either about the immortality of the soul or the resurrection of the dead...." But, he adds, this is "quite unlike anything that can be called orthodox Christian belief...."[1]

Although on one level this all sounds so wonderful, the big question is whether it is true. On what basis do we reach these conclusions? Is this the product of our own wishful thinking, or do we have some objective footing on which to base these ideas?

Then we have the issue of justice. God may be a God of love, but how does justice fit into this equation? If He is a just God, how could He welcome someone as evil as Adolf Hitler into heaven with open arms after "the fuhrer" murdered six million Jews? Think of the others who have caused so much misery and death. Joseph Stalin, Pol Pot, Idi Amin, Mao Tse-tung, and Osama bin Laden, to name just a few. What about the terrorists whose bombs kill and maim innocent children? Mass murderers and serial killers? Should they simply be forgiven and welcomed into heaven, completely pardoned for their crimes even though they have never shown the slightest bit of remorse nor asked for forgiveness?

Yet people say, "Surely we can't believe in hell in this enlightened age." And, "I just can't imagine a loving God sending anyone to hell."

Here is a fact I bet you didn't know: the Bible, especially the New Testament, has more to say about hell than heaven. That's right—there are more pages of Scripture devoted to hell than to heaven! That is why I felt I needed to thoroughly cover the topic of hell as well as heaven when talking about the afterlife. That's why I interviewed people who claim to have experienced the torments of hell as well as the pleasures of heaven. I wanted to treat the whole subject as objectively and thoroughly as possible.

I don't want to believe in hell. I wish it wasn't real, and that there was no need for it. But my experience as a human being convinces me that hell is necessary, and my years of theological study have strengthened my belief.

I heard a story about a battleship that was making its way through foggy waters off the coast of California. The captain was startled when he saw a light cutting through the darkness ahead. Another vessel seemed to be heading directly toward his ship.

He immediately got on the radio and ordered the other ship, "Alter your course ten degrees south! Over."

To his amazement, he received what he took to be a belligerent reply. "Please alter your course ten degrees north. Over."

"I am a captain!" he thundered. "Alter your course."

"I'm a private," came the reply. "But with all due respect, I must ask you to alter your course ten degrees north."

The captain was beside himself. Who did this arrogant private think he was? He would have this fellow court martialed.

"Private," he shouted, "I am a battleship!"

"I understand, sir," came the reply. "But I am a lighthouse."

That changed everything. The captain sheepishly began changing his ship's course, as the private had asked.

My belief is that the Bible is like a lighthouse in that it contains God's truth. If someone needs a course correction, it's us, not Him. If we disregard what He says, we are likely to wind up broken on the rocks along the shore. The Bible says that heaven and hell are real, so I accept that this is true. No other proof is necessary for me. And yet, such proof is all around us.

THERE IS EVIL IN THE WORLD

For example, in my role as president and CEO of Jewish Voice Ministries, I have traveled into some of the remotest parts of the world. I have been in areas that seem to be held hostage by superstition and fear, where oppression is palpable. I've seen groups bitterly oppressed and persecuted simply because of who they were or what they believed.

I've witnessed unreasoning hate in the eyes of people who despised me for no other reason than the fact that I am a Jew. I have been spit on and cursed at, simply because of my heritage. Adolf Hitler is long dead and gone, but the evil that drove him is still present in the world today. I've been rejected and despised by others simply because I believe in God and share my faith openly.

I work extensively in countries including India and Ethiopia where death and disease are widespread and suffering is great. I've seen little children die from malnutrition and polluted water. I've been in countries ruled by brutal dictators who have slaughtered masses of their own people to retain control.

Yes, there is evil in the world. A person would have to be blind not to see it. I believe that the presence of evil people in our world reveals that there are also unseen forces of evil. In other words, my own experience has deepened my convictions that just as there is a personal God who created us and loves us, there is an evil adversary, Satan, who is out to destroy us—to make life a hell on earth and deceive us into believing…or rather *not* believing in the existence of an eternal hell.

For many centuries, most people in the Western world believed that when they died they would either go to heaven or hell. But as the industrial revolution spread around the world—and the United States—a belief in the afterlife began to wane. It seemed to many that advancing technologies would make it possible for humankind to build their own heaven right here on earth. And "enlightened" attitudes caused many people, even pastors, to rethink their positions on hell. Poet Emily Dickinson wistfully addressed these changes in thinking in an untitled poem:

Those dying then,
Knew where they went—
They went to God's Right Hand—
That Hand is amputated now
And God cannot be found.

The abdication of Belief
Makes the Behavior small—
Better an ignis fatuus
Than no illume at all—

In their book *Jonathan Edwards on Heaven & Hell,* Owen Strachan and Douglas Sweeney write:

> Many who do believe in Christianity have modernized it. We have made our faith about fulfillment and achievement, sentimentalized love and earthly progress. We have adopted the consumerist mind-set of the West and have substituted the pursuit of plenty for the pursuit of piety.[2]

And yet, as Terry Scott Taylor wrote in his "Skeptic's Song," "It won't turn the temperature one degree, simply because you don't believe…."[3]

Whether we believe in hell doesn't make the least bit of difference as to whether it really exists. The same is true of heaven.

Although I attempt to be objective and thorough on the subject of the afterlife, this is not going to be a book about hell. That's only part of the picture. Talking about hell is the most difficult task I face in writing this book, so I wanted to get it out into the open immediately.

HEAVEN IS FOR REAL

The good news is that I'm also convinced heaven is real, and that the glories of heaven are made even more magnificent and thrilling because of the existence of hell—just as life's best moments are made sweeter by the times of sorrow we've endured.

And although I came to believe in a literal heaven and hell after discovering over three decades ago that the Bible is true, my faith has been strengthened by meeting and hearing the stories of people who've been close enough to get a glimpse of paradise. I have also talked to those who witnessed the horrors of hell. Of course, the things I've heard from them cannot be scientifically proved or disproved. Those who are inclined to believe will believe, regardless of any skepticism or doubt they encounter. Those inclined to disbelieve will do so, regardless of whatever proof they are given. And yet, there are thousands, if not more, who have crossed the threshold of death and come back to share their experiences.

One of the best known of these is Colton Burpo, whose story was told in the best-selling book and movie *Heaven Is for Real*. The movie, released in the spring of 2014, starred Greg Kinnear as Colton's father, Todd, a pastor who wrote the book about his son's adventures in heaven. It ranked among the top five movies at the box office for nearly two months and, as of July 2014, had earned more than $90 million within the United States.

Colton Burpo was four years of age when he underwent an emergency appendectomy. Although seriously ill, there was never a time during the procedure when Colton's heart stopped or he was declared dead. But later, as he recovered, he began to talk about what had happened to him during the time when he was in the hospital, fighting for his life.

He told of floating above his body, looking down on the doctors and nurses who were operating him. He saw his father in the hospital chapel, "yelling at God," something the pastor sheepishly admits he was probably doing. Colton also told of meeting Jesus who took him to heaven where he saw many angels and met his grandfather and a sister he didn't know he had. (Colton had no idea that his parents had lost a little girl to a miscarriage.)

There is much more to the story, but instead of going into it here, I'll just suggest that you read the book for yourself if you haven't already.

Heaven Is for Real is one of many books on Near-Death Experiences (NDEs) that have captured the public's attention and generated a huge amount of discussion about life after death. Another bestseller is *Proof of Heaven,* written by neurosurgeon Eben Alexander. His book, which hit number one on *The New York Times* best-seller list, is subtitled, *A Scientist's Case for the Afterlife.* It presents a rather New Age view of the life beyond this one, and certain aspects of Dr. Alexander's story have been questioned in a lengthy article in *Esquire* magazine. Other recent books include *To Heaven and Back* by surgeon Mary C. Neal, who was once director of spine surgery at the University of Southern California; *The Boy Who Came Back from Heaven* by Kevin and Alex Malarkey; and *90 Minutes in Heaven* by well-known Baptist pastor Don Piper, who went to heaven after he "died" in an automobile accident on January 18, 1989.

But not every Near-Death Experience has been happy. "Earthquake" Kelley wrote of his descent into hell in *Bound to Lose Destined to Win.* Bill Wiese made the best-seller lists with his *23 Minutes in Hell,* and former atheist Howard Storm, now a Christian minister, gave his readers plenty of goose bumps in his chilling book, *My Descent into Death*.

There are numerous other books on the topic, and the content is all over the map. Some are well-written and thoughtful. Others are just the opposite. Some have the ring of authenticity, while others sound like poorly devised fiction. Some are consistent with what the Scriptures teach, while others are filled with New Age teachings.

The reaction to the books has been interesting. Some people are ready to believe everything. Some won't believe anything, no matter how compelling the evidence might be.

Obviously, all of these authors can't all be telling the truth. Either some of them are lying, or they've been lied to. We need to be discerning—our future, eternal future depends on it.

Because of the keen interest these authors provoked, and also because of the extreme importance of the subject of life after death, I spent more than a year investigating the claims of those who wrote about their NDEs. With the help of a full-time researcher, I contacted and interviewed more than a dozen of these people who claimed to have tasted the afterlife. My goal was to find a common thread in the best of the accounts and to discover what all of these people had in common after their experiences. Those who seemed most believable, and whose stories held up under close scrutiny, were invited to appear as guests on my television show, *Jewish Voice with Jonathan Bernis*, as part of a series on the afterlife.

The best of these interviews challenged and strengthened my faith. I was inspired to hear first-person accounts of the glories that await us in heaven—and distraught by the testimonies of those who witnessed the horrors of a literal hell. Although I have believed in heaven and hell a long time, conducting these interviews made both eternal destinations seem more vividly real and renewed my passion for making sure people get to heaven and avoid any possibility of going to hell. As previously mentioned, I'll present six of the near-death accounts that most impressed me.

A Brief History of Near-Death Experiences

Accounts of Near-Death Experiences reach far back into ancient history. One of the earliest comes to us through the philosopher Plato, who described the story of a man named Er in his famous treatise, *The Republic*. The so-called "Myth of Er" is worth examining in detail for its early confirmation of the belief in heaven and hell.

Er, a Greek soldier, was killed in battle. His body was about to be thrown onto a funeral pyre when he suddenly revived. Soon thereafter, he told the tale of his amazing journey into the afterlife. Accompanied by a host of other souls, Er arrived at a meadow dominated by four great openings—two into and out of the sky, and two into and out of the earth. Seated at the entrance to these openings were four judges who directed each soul to the path they were to follow—the good, to the path in the sky, the evil to the path leading deep into the earth.

As Er approached the judgment seat, he was held back by the sages and told to listen, observe, and subsequently report his experience to humanity. As he beheld in wonder, radiant souls floated down from the sky, telling tales of sublime pleasures and ecstatic emotions. Others, meanwhile, emerged from within the earth, filthy, frightened, and weeping with despair as they recounted the terrible experiences they had undergone there.

Plato's account of Er's adventure greatly influenced religious, philosophical, and scientific thought for many centuries to come, although it wasn't until 1890 that the term "Near-Death Experience" was first used by French psychologist Victor Egger. He used the words to describe accounts he had heard from mountain climbers who saw their lives flash before their eyes during near-fatal falls. The similarities in the climber's accounts intrigued the doctor, but it would not be until almost a century later that any systematic attempt was made to catalog the characteristics that comprised the experience.

In 1975, American psychiatrist Raymond Moody conducted groundbreaking work in defining and isolating the elements of Near-Death Experiences. He and other researchers developed a working definition of these events as a personal experience associated with impending death. The experience included a number of sensations including detachment from the body, feelings of levitation, total serenity, as well as security, warmth, absolute dissolution, and the often reported presence of a welcoming light.

The phenomena most often occurred after the subject had been pronounced clinically dead or was very close to dying. Small wonder, then, that modern developments in cardiac resuscitation and other lifesaving techniques have substantially increased the reported incidents of Near-Death Experiences.

Researchers found that a classic Near-Death Experience includes the following:

- An awareness of being dead.

- An out-of-body experience, including the perception of viewing one's body from an elevated position. This includes occasional reports of observing doctors and nurses attempting medical resuscitation efforts.

- The so-called "tunnel experience," a sense of moving up a passageway or staircase.

- A movement toward a powerful light, often culminating in a sudden immersion in the light and a sense of communing with the spirit that inhabited the light. This included encountering "Beings of Light," often dressed in white robes. These beings sometimes were identified as deceased loved ones.

- An overwhelming sense of unconditional love.

- Having one's life reviewed in intense and accurate detail. This sensation of having one's life "flash before your eyes" is sometimes accompanied by profound revelations of the past and even the nature of the universe.

- The rapid approach of what has been described as a "border" or boundary line, sometimes accompanied by discordant sounds and noises.

Popular interest in NDE was sparked by the publication in 1975 of Dr. Moody's best-selling book *Life After Life,* which prompted the founding of the International Association for Near Death Studies in 1981.

Life After Life presented a number of case studies, all of which recounted pleasant, happy, welcome dying experiences. No one, it seemed, returned from "the other side" with stories of frightening experiences or fearful encounters. The consensus was that being dead was much preferable to life here on this mortal plain.

So much for hell.

Then, in 1986, a cardiologist by the name of Maurice Rawlings published a book called *Beyond Death's Door,* in which he presented a number of case studies where people had undergone NDEs that can only be described as hellish.

The first time it happened, Dr. Rawlings was attempting to resuscitate a patient who had suffered a near-fatal heart attack. During the procedure, the patient was extremely agitated and began grabbing at him and shouting in terror, "Help me! I'm in hell! Get me out of here!" Fortunately for the patient, Dr. Rawlings was able to save his life. As soon as the man had recovered enough to be able to talk about his experience, Dr. Rawlings went to his hospital room and asked him what he had been screaming about.

Much to Rawlings' surprise, the recovering patient had no idea what the doctor was talking about. He remembered nothing at all about being in hell or calling for help. The whole experience was blacked out. Could it be that it was too terrible to remember, that the man's mind simply refused to go back there? Or was there something else at play? Dr. Rawlings could not forget the man's cries for help nor the look of terror on his face. He had no doubt that something terrible had been happening to him.

This experience changed Dr. Rawlings' life. A lifelong atheist, he became a devout Christian. He also began his own research into Near-Death Experiences, which included asking other resuscitated patients about their experiences before they had time to forget them. He used these as the basis for four books on NDEs, recounting both pleasurable and terrifying experiences.

Subsequent to *Life After Life*, Dr. Moody also recorded some negative NDEs in his book, *The Light Beyond*, which was published in 1988.

One man recalls seeing, "a lot of people down there, screaming, howling...almost a million.... They were miserable and hateful. They were asking me for water."[4]

Moody also reports that a young man who attempted to commit suicide experienced: "...images of some horrific beings clutching and clawing at him. It was something like descending into Dante's inferno. He had a claustrophobic, hostile, nightmarish NDE, without the slightest positive experience...no being of light, nothing beautiful, nothing pleasant."[5]

Meanwhile, a substantial number of doctors, scientists, and specialists continue to insist that the Near-Death Experience, far from providing proof of the afterlife, is simply a chemical and biological reaction to the experience of dying—the so-called "Dying Brain Syndrome." The cause of the vivid "visions" that accompany the events have been attributed to everything from plunging blood pressure; a surge of electrical activity as the brain runs out oxygen just prior to expiration; a previous use of psychedelic drugs by the subjects; a "dissociative defense mechanism that occurs in times of extreme danger"; or what has been termed a "global stroke of the brain."

What is, however, virtually impossible to explain in detached scientific terminology is the profound change in values and virtues undergone by many subjects who have undergone the Near-Death Experience. These include, but are not limited to, a greater appreciation for life, higher self-esteem, greater compassion for others, a heightened sense of purpose and self-understanding, a desire to learn, elevated spirituality, greater ecological sensitivity and planetary concern, and a feeling of being more intuitive. Changes may also include a feeling that the brain has been "altered" to encompass more and a sensation that one is now using the "whole brain" rather than a small part.

These profound changes are strong evidence for the belief that the Near-Death Experience is, in fact, a foretaste of the afterlife. What, after all, could affect a more complete change of character and worldview than an encounter with eternity?

Science has no explanation for those individuals who, once having been resuscitated, have gone on to live lives that are often in stark contrast to their previous ethics and value systems.

Regardless of the varied, and sometimes contradictory, biological and physiological causes to which the Near-Death Experience has been attributed, there has as yet been no purely physical explanation for these events. Science, in short, is woefully inadequate in explaining a phenomenon that seems to establish that human consciousness can function independently of measurable brain activity.

In his book *To Hell and Back,* Dr. Maurice Rawlings writes:

> Secular Skeptics…conveniently dismiss the whole near-death experience as the product of hallucination from chemical change in the oxygen-deprived mind. Unfortunately, experiments with the oxygen deprived mind do not produce these findings. In fact, the

hallucination theory cannot account for a whole list of things found in bona fide experiences: the power of transcendency, experiences that occur in another world, positive visual reconstruction of events at the scene of the emergency, the remarkable reproducibility of sequences, or the resulting miraculous change or turn-around in people's lifestyles.[6]

Some researchers have tried to verify whether the spirit actually separates from the body during Near-Death Experiences. In her book *Testing the Spirits,* Elizabeth L. Hillstrom tells of work done by a cardiologist named Michael Sabom. Dr. Sabom interviewed people who said they had watched doctors fighting to save their lives during NDE and asked them describe what they saw. He then went back and compared their accounts with the medical records. According to Hillstrom, "Sabom found that there was quite a bit of consistency between the medical records and NDE accounts and no obvious discrepancies."[7] The doctor then interviewed 24 patients who had undergone multiple resuscitations but reported no NDE. He asked these people to imagine they were watching a resuscitation attempt and describe what happened.

> In this group, twenty-two of the twenty-five made at least one major error in their descriptions, and the three who didn't make any errors gave only very general accounts. By way of contrast, twenty-six out of thirty-two NDErs gave general visual impressions with no errors, while six gave unique, specific details that could be verified by medical records.[8]

Sabom found that 13 other patients who had experienced a NDE were able to provide "impressive visual details of their surgeries that they probably should not have known." Hillstrom concludes:

> Sabom's work does not prove that NDEs produce real separation of body and spirit, but it does strongly suggest that something unusual is happening. If his conclusions are correct, some of his patients did acquire visual impressions of the medical procedures that were being used on them while, by all physical indications, they should have been completely unconscious.[9]

Dinesh D'Souza notes:

> Most of the critics of NDEs are atheists who recognize the potency and persuasive power of this research [into the NDE experience] and have raised a multitude of objections. Strictly speaking, this is true. No corpses have risen out of coffins to deliver surprise orations at their funerals.... Even so, the criticism seems to be based on a quibble. We are trying to elicit information about what comes after death, and if we cannot get such information from those who are actually dead, then our best bet is to get it from those who are nearest to the edge. So "near death" isn't "dead," but it is as close as we are likely to get.[10]

While some of those I interviewed did not actually die, but did claim to have out of body experiences, others did die and were dead for rather long periods of time. More on this in Part Four.

CHRISTIAN OPPOSITION

The study of Near-Death Experiences has also received opposition from some fundamentalist Christian leaders who believe that the study of what happens after death is "off limits" for believing Christians and will only lead to deception. Well-known pastor and teacher John MacArthur writes:

> There's no point in probing and dissecting people's near-death experiences, as if they would give us some important truth about the Afterlife that we are lacking from Scripture. What Scripture teaches us about Heaven, angels, and the Afterlife is sufficient and accurate. God has already given us everything we need to know to equip us for every good work. (2 Tim. 3:17) There's nothing an eyewitness testimony could reliably add.[11]

I humbly disagree. I believe there is value in looking at NDEs because they affirm for us that there really is a life beyond this one. They help us maintain a proper perspective, an understanding that this life is only the beginning, and the things we do now can literally impact us for eternity. I also believe that God, in His mercy, is allowing us to hear some of these accounts because they shake us out of our complacency and motivate us to live with meaning and purpose, with eternity in focus.

I do agree with MacArthur that, "Clearly, because Scripture is the Word of God, we must reject every anecdotal account that contradicts what Scripture teaches."[12] We can never accept personal experience that contradicts what the Bible teaches. When the word of a human being collides with the Word of God, the Word of God should always prevail. We must always base any and all testimony on the revealed truth of Scripture.

I admit that it is possible that some of these experiences may be delusions, deceptions that seek to fool us into thinking that after we die we will experience bliss and joy, no matter how we conduct ourselves, or believe, in this world. *What we do and believe in this life does matter.*

Dr. Rawlings tells of his conversation with a young man who was donating blood at a blood bank. The husky white male, about 21 years of age, had three recently healed bullet wounds in his chest.

Realizing that the wounds could be a source of infection in the blood, Rawlings started asking questions about the bullet wounds. The young man explained that he had been shot by a cross-dresser he had beaten. Rawlings writes, "He told me the residual bullet wounds in his chest required both resuscitation from coma and blood transfusions. Three small caliber bullets had entered the left chest, one of them nicking the heart wall at the time."

The blood donor explained that he was no stranger to violence, and even admitted that he had killed a couple in an armed robbery three years earlier. Then he told an even more amazing story.

Rawlings says, "During CPR in the ambulance, he told me he had an out-of-body experience. He was surprised by the heavenly light surrounding him. He felt welcomed by the light. The light was 'understanding.' No ridicule or rejection. The sordid parts of his life were not examined…Only 'peace and love' were communicated."

When Rawlings asked him how he felt about this, the fellow said, "Well, it felt good to be in this beautiful place, you know, but I kept wondering why the light never asked me about beating the heck out of the cross-dresser. And the light never mentioned the two killings from the past. I was glad he didn't ask me about those things, but if he was from God, why didn't he? …I knew I should be in hell instead of this place, but I kept quiet." Dr. Rawlings concludes, "Looking around and lowering his voice, he said, 'Doc, does God ever make mistakes?' This report helped crystallize my thinking. It was evident that Satan very often masquerades as God, and that one simply must analyze reports to discern if the 'being of light' is from God or not."[13]

And, of course, we have to be careful not to become obsessed with Near-Death Experiences, or trying to figure out what lies beyond the other side of death. The Bible is very clear that we are not to attempt to communicate with the dead, seek guidance from the dead, or take part in séances or other occult practices. (See Leviticus 19:31, 20:6 and 20:27.)

Still, I believe there are many reasons why God may allow us a brief glimpse of the afterlife.

In *To Hell and Back,* Dr. Rawlings repeats a story told by Dr. Diane Komp, a professor of pediatrics at Yale University. Dr. Komp was at the bedside of a seven-year-old girl who was dying of leukemia. "The little girl managed the final energy to sit up and say, 'The angels—they're so beautiful! Mommy, do you see them? I've never heard such beautiful singing.' Then she died." Dr. Komp said, "The word that most closely describes what I felt is 'gift.' It wasn't just that the child was given the gift of peace in the moment of her death, but that this was a gift to her parents."[14]

Many of those who've had Near-Death Experiences believe that one reason they were sent back to this life was to share their stories. If this is so, then it could be that these personal accounts of heaven and hell are a gift from God, meant to comfort us, encourage us, and at the same time to disturb and warn us. To illuminate our path and help us prepare for what lies ahead.

We'll talk more about NDEs when we get to the final section of this book. But first I want to spend some time talking about the place all of us hope to end up one day.

Come with me to heaven.

Part Two

HEAVEN

Chapter 3

LOOKING FOR PARADISE

DO YOU BELIEVE IN heaven?

If so, you're in good company. According to an ABC News poll undertaken in December 2005, nearly 90 percent of Americans believe in heaven and almost all of these think they're going to go there when they die. (On the other side of the picture, a Barna Group poll in October 2013 found that less than one half of 1 percent of all Americans believe they are doomed to hell.)

What about Near-Death Experiences? Have you had one, or know someone who has? A *U.S. News and World Report* survey in the late 1990s found that as many as 18 million Americans believe they have had experiences that gave them a glimpse of the afterlife. The number has increased since then, as confirmed by the large number of best-selling books written by people who claim to have had such a life-changing experience.

Despite the fact that most Americans believe in heaven—and a lot of us feel that we've had at least a glimpse of it—we don't always agree on what it looks like, how to get there, or what's going to happen if and when we do get there.

George Barna, the well-known Christian pollster, found that 10 percent of Bible-believing Christians, who believe they will get into heaven solely because of their faith in Jesus, also believe in reincarnation. He also says that 29 percent of Christians believe it is possible to communicate with the dead, and 50 percent say it is possible to earn salvation based upon good works.

Barna writes:

> Many committed born again Christians believe that people have multiple options for gaining entry into Heaven... Millions of Americans have redefined grace to mean that God is so eager to save people from Hell that He will change His nature and universal principles for their individual benefit. It is astounding how many people develop their faith according to their feelings or cultural assumptions rather than biblical teachings.[1]

What is the truth? How do we get to heaven? What will we find when we get there? And what does heaven look like?

A Brief History of Heaven

Nearly every culture in every period of history has had a belief in some sort of heaven, although those beliefs differed a great deal from one society to the next. For example, the Vikings believed they would spend eternity feasting, drinking, and occasionally brawling in Valhalla. Romans thought their souls would ride into heaven on a fiery chariot. Far Eastern religions spoke of Nirvana, where the soul is subjected to a constant cycle of birth and rebirth.

Ancient Egyptians thought that the soul of the departed would travel on a perilous journey to paradise. Along the way, he or she would have to do battle with supernatural beings. In order to prepare the dead for their journey to the other world, the Egyptians equipped their graves with everything they would need to make the trip, including food, weapons, and gifts for the gods. Even so, defeating the supernatural beings did not guarantee the departed soul a place in paradise. According to Egyptian lore, the spiritual traveler would be judged worthy of entrance into paradise only after his heart was weighed. If a scintilla of sin was detected, the unfortunate soul's heart would be devoured by demons.

Although I'll talk more about Jewish beliefs concerning the afterlife in the next chapter, I do want to mention here that the Jews had a very different view of death than did the Egyptians, and most other ancient cultures. Rather than filling tombs with luxuries to be used in the world beyond, Jews buried their loved ones in simple coffins and shrouds without pockets to symbolize that none of a man's material possessions could be taken with him after death. Jews believed that "in the hour of man's departure from this world, neither gold, nor precious stones nor pearls accompany him but only Torah and good works."[2]

In addition to this, some 1,800 years ago, Rabbi Gamaliel instituted the practice of burying all Jews in the same type of simple shroud made of inexpensive cotton, muslin, or linen, to show that no matter how rich or poor they may be in this life, ultimately, all people are equal before God.[3]

Buddhist teachings speak of several heavens. A warrior who fights for good will enter a realm called the "Devas of Passionate Delight" where he will be rewarded for doing battle. A comic actor who makes audiences laugh will enter into the realm of the "Laughing Devas." In Tibetan Buddhism, the categories are even more complex. There are, for instance, no less than four separate heavens of Formless Spirits, six heavens of Resplendent Sensuality, and a total of sixteen heavens free from sensuality. The faithful Buddhist who accumulates good karma may dwell in one of these paradises, but not forever. Eventually, his or her good karma will be depleted and he or she will return to earth to start the process all over again.

For Hindus, heaven is closely related to the physical world. They perceive paradise as imperfect, a place simply for fleshly and pleasurable pursuits, and a dwelling place for their teeming pantheon of gods, a so-called Good Kingdom ruled over by the beneficent King of Devas. For the devout Hindu, the goal of existence is not to reside forever in this kingdom but to achieve *Moksha*, a final and complete transcendence of all earthly desires and cares.

Islam teaches a far different doctrine. The Koran speaks in numerous places of an afterlife in "Eden" for all those who live according to its precepts. In verse 35 of the Surah Al-Ra'd, the Islamic holy book describes heaven thusly: "Beneath it flows rivers. Perpetual is the fruits thereof and the shade therein. Such is the End of the Righteous; and the end of the unbelievers is the Fire."

Islamic believers perceive heaven as a physical place, a lush paradise where their every wish is instantly granted. Those who dwell there are attired in rich garb and eat sumptuous feasts while reclining on couches inlaid with gold and diamonds. In an echo of the ancient practice of ancestor worship, the believer will rejoice in the company of his departed relatives. The more good deeds one performs on earth, the higher level of heaven is open to him or her, with the highest of all being the fabled Seventh Heaven, where palaces built by angels for the faithful are constructed of solid gold.

Imam Feisal Abdul Rauf, founder of the American Society for Muslim Advancement, shared his view of heaven with ABC's Barbara Walters. "We are all told we will be in comfortable homes, reclining on silk couches…so we're given the delights of sex, the delights of wine, the delights of food with all of their positive things without their negative aspects."[4]

The list goes on. For some people of the South Pacific, heaven is part of the universe shaped like a coconut. As with many primitive religions, paradise is divided into distinct neighborhoods: there is a heaven of sunshine and rain, one of newborn children, and one where human souls are created. The entire cosmos is, in turn, supported by pillars anchored to the bottom of the sea.

JUST A DREAM…OR REALITY?

Dr. Reggie Anderson tells of talking with a patient who recovered after being dead for two hours. The woman had flat-lined while undergoing a procedure to open a blockage of the left anterior descending artery of her heart. Two hours later, "her heart kicked in and started beating by itself." Three days later, Dr. Anderson's patient was out of a coma and feeling just fine. Here's what she told him.

> The last thing I remember was lying on that table while they did something to my heart. Then, suddenly there was a lot of commotion. People were yelling and

handing medical equipment back and forth. I knew they were working on my shell. They said I died on that table. That I was dead for two hours! But I don't remember it because I wasn't there on that table. I was somewhere else where I was more alive than I've ever been. It was peaceful there, and calm, very different from here, and the exact opposite of the craziness that was going on where my body lay on that table. A sensation of total peace enveloped me, and I felt as though I was floating.

I didn't feel any more pain. Even before my heart attack, I always had pain, what with the arthritis and the neuropathy. But now, I no longer had that burning in my legs; in fact, they felt strong. For the first time in three years, I stood up and walked without a wheelchair or a walker.

I walked down a path next to a stream. I could feel an icy spray blowing on me as I passed. I stopped to take a drink, and the water was as fresh and cold as an Alaskan stream, but the water was sweet—it tasted like honey.

When I looked around I saw an astounding array of colors, and the pigments seemed so concentrated! It was more colorful than anything I'd ever seen or imagined.

I walked around a bend in the path, and I saw an open field with the greenest grass—I've never seen that color of grass before! Right in the middle of that meadow stood a horse-drawn carriage! My father loved horses. Seeing that beautiful animal with its gleaming coat reminded me of him...

Suddenly, my view was blocked. A crowd of people stood in front of the carriage. I looked closer, and I saw my father, my sweet mother, and my dear brother! They died years ago! In fact, I recognized people in the crowd who had passed away decades ago. But when I saw them, it was if no time had passed at all. It was as though our spirits were united with an understanding that defied words. In fact, I'm not sure we even used words to communicate.[5]

Is she telling the truth? Was she describing a lucid dream, or reality? Her doctor believes her story. What about you?

There was a time—not too long ago—when science insisted that heaven could not exist. There was no room for a place like heaven in a universe made of physical matter, and every action was completely predictable based on laws of motion, mass, velocity, and so forth. The human body is a physical object. After death, it decays. Scientific observation showed that life ends at death.

Enter quantum physics. As Dinesh D'Souza writes, "This revolution, which represents the transition from classical to modern physics, involved a complete reformulation of the laws of space, time and matter...." He adds, "Far from undermining the chances for life after death, modern physics undermines the premises of materialism. Moreover, new discoveries in physics provide scenarios under which matter can survive with different properties in realms other than our universe. Fantastic though it sounds, modern physics has legitimated the possibility of the afterlife."[6]

Some of the realities that quantum physics has discovered make no sense at all under old Newtonian physics. For example, it is possible for a particle to leave an area before it ever gets there. A particle can be in two or more places at the same time. And even stranger, some particles behave differently if they are being observed.

Quantum physics also suggests that there are many different universes. Ours is just one of them, which means that the reality we know is only one of many possible realities. As D'Souza says:

> Modern physics has expanded our horizons and shown how life after death is possible within an existing framework of physical reality. The materialist objection has proved to be a dud; in fact, modern physics calls materialism itself into question. In a crucial area, and sometimes against the intentions of the scientists themselves, modern science has proven itself not the foe of religious believers, but an unexpected ally.[7]

WHICH HEAVEN IS REAL?

Given this complex and contradictory catalog of possible paradises, it is no wonder many are confused about what to believe. Which of the myriad versions of heaven is real? Or are they all simply the fanciful projections of human imagination? Nothing more than myths? And, if heaven is real, which one? If so many cultures and religions throughout history have believed so many different variations of heaven, who is right? Or, maybe they're all right. Maybe heaven is however you envision it?

The danger here, as mentioned previously, is subjective reality. Just believing something does not make it real or true. We cannot simply believe or will something to be if it is not real to begin with, if it is not part of a created order. Not if we believe in a Creator and some form of divine order that is responsible for what we see. We cannot simply create a heaven from our own imagination and then rely on that creation to become our reality.

The question then becomes…is there a source we can turn to for accurate information, for insight, for direction? Is there a "textbook" provided to us by the Creator, a "user guide" that establishes *absolute truth?* I believe there is—the Holy Scriptures. And it is from the revelation contained in this book—a book I was raised with as a Jew and concluded over 30 years ago was the true Word of God—that convinces me that yes, there is an indescribably beautiful heaven waiting for us.

This same book lays out a very specific plan, with very specific instructions, on what we must do and believe in order to enter this paradise. And, according to those Scriptures, "the road is narrow and few find it."[8]

If this book, the Bible, is in fact the Word of God and gives us the "correct" information about heaven and the afterlife, then we should begin with "the People of Book"—the Jews. Since God called Abraham more than 4,000 years ago and promised to make him into a great nation, the Jews have been charged with the responsibility of bringing the revelation of the One True God to the world. The entire Bible, both Old and New Testaments (with the exceptions of perhaps the books of Luke and Acts) was given to us by the Jewish people. So let's look now at what their sages and Scriptures have to tell us about this place called heaven.

Chapter 4

Ancient and Modern Jewish Views of Heaven

Do Jews BELIEVE THAT the righteous will live forever in heaven?

Yes.

And no.

In other words, some do, and some don't—and it's been that way for thousands of years.

It's not surprising that some Jews don't believe in life after death. As I mentioned earlier, it's possible to be a Jew in good standing and not even believe in God—although this hasn't always been the case. And if you don't believe in God, you most likely won't believe in heaven.

The reason for the wide variety of Jewish views about the afterlife is that there is such diversity of belief within Judaism. Many Jews are now secular and would define their beliefs as agnostic.

Others are devout atheists. Some practice Eastern religions and believe in karma or reincarnation. In fact, you can believe in just about everything or nothing in Judaism and still be a "good" Jew... except perhaps in Jesus.

Even among the orthodox (those who strictly adhere to Jewish law and heritage) we find a myriad of views on the afterlife. This is because there is not one definitive teaching on life after death in the Talmud, Midrash, or other rabbinical writings. Instead, these books contain many different points of view on the subject. Before I get to a few examples of this, let me briefly explain how the Talmud and the Midrash were compiled.

As I wrote in my book *A Rabbi Looks at Jesus of Nazareth*:

> If one man should be singled out as the founder of Rabbinic Judaism, it would be Rabbi Yochanan ben Zakkai. He was the first president of the Rabbinical academy at Yabneh, which was established soon after the destruction of the Temple by the Romans in 70 A.D..... The rabbis believed that two sets of laws, equally important, had been given to Moses at Mount Sinai. The first was the Torah, the first five books of the Tanakh (Old Testament), which were written by Moses. The second was the oral law, which, according to their tradition, was given to Moses with the Torah at Mount Sinai.[1]

After the destruction of the temple, it was at Yabneh that a council convened to discuss the future of Judaism. With the temple gone, Jews could no longer offer animal sacrifices in order to have their sins forgiven. Ben Zakkai pointed to Hosea 6:6 as an indication that God no longer required such sacrifices. The passage says,

"For I desire mercy, not sacrifice, and acknowledgment of God rather than burnt offerings." The rabbis reasoned that, because God had allowed the temple to be destroyed, He no longer desired burnt offerings from His people.

Ben Zakkai and the other rabbis gathered at Yabneh were confronted by some serious issues. First, the war with Rome had left the nation in ruins and killed half a million of their people. Second, a new "sect" of Jews who embraced Yeshua of Nazareth as the Messiah (which later came to be known as Christianity) was rapidly spreading across the land. The rabbis were determined to stop this threat to their authority.

One way they tried to do this was by banning the Septuagint, the Greek translation of the Tanakh, which was used by most of those who had accepted Yeshua as Messiah. By labeling the Greek translations as impure, the council sought to discredit these Jewish believers in the eyes of their countrymen. This was a strange thing to do because Greek was the lingua franca of first-century Palestine. Most Jewish people could read Greek, but not Hebrew.

As I wrote in my previous book:

> Most historians will tell you that Rabbinic Judaism pre-dated the council at Yabneh. The belief in two equally important Laws—one written, the other oral—had been around for centuries. However, the council played a pivotal role in elevating this form of Judaism into the prevailing religion of Israel.
>
> This is still the Judaism that reigns today. Of the estimated 13.3 million Jews in the world, only a handful of

those who are observant practice some form other than Rabbinic Judaism. One group, called the Karaites, accept only the written Torah as their guide in matters of faith and practice. Although the Karaites were once a significant force in worldwide Judaism, only an estimated 30,000 of them survive today. Clearly, Rabbinic Judaism has won out in the battle for the allegiance of the Jewish people....[2]

With the temple gone, rabbinical interpretations of Scripture and Jewish law became increasingly important. Most likely beginning with the council in Yabneh, rabbis began to commit the oral law to writing, compiling what became known as the Mishnah. Over the next few hundred years, the Mishnah was further developed and served as the basis for the Talmud.

The Talmud, which is Hebrew for "study," explains in painstaking detail how the commandments of the Torah are to be carried out. For example, the Torah teaches that no one is to work on the Sabbath, but isn't totally clear as to what constitutes work and what doesn't. The Talmudic tractate *Shabbat* devotes an entire chapter to a discussion of which types of work are prohibited and which are permitted.

Actually, there are two Talmuds. The Jerusalem Talmud from Palestine and the Babylonian Talmud, which was edited in what is present-day Iraq. The Jerusalem Talmud is the older of the two, but the Babylonian Talmud is generally considered to be more authoritative and comprehensive.

Rabbi Y'hudah HaNasi (Judah the Prince), who was leader of the Jewish community in Palestine at the beginning of the third century, is thought to be the editor of the sixty-three tractates of the

Mishnah. Rav Ashi, who spent over fifty years collecting the material, is considered the primary editor of the Gemara, which is the second part of the Talmud—primarily consisting of commentary on the Mishnah.

Here's how the Talmud works. A law from the Mishnah is recorded, followed by rabbinic deliberations on its meaning. Sometimes the rabbis ramble, take circuitous paths to their goal, and wander far off track. Pretty much anything that was of interest to these rabbis found its way into the Talmud. And, as I've mentioned before, there is no consensus. Rabbis often disagree with one another and debate rages. Which point of view is correct? That's left up to the reader to decide.

Together, the Torah, the Talmud, and other rabbinic writings make up what is called Halakhah, the totality of Jewish law. Halakhah is filled with rules and practices that impact every area of a person's life. Detailed instructions are provided on what you are to do when you first wake up in the morning—what to eat, what to wear, how to cut your hair—just about anything else you can imagine.

The Talmud that we have today was completed around the 7th century A.D. The Midrash, which is a lengthy commentary on the Talmud, was written over hundreds of years. Together, the Talmud and the Midrash contain thousands of pages of laws, instructions, interpretations of scriptures, parables, debates, and proverbs. The pages are filled with contradictory points of view on just about every subject—including what happens after death.

The Rabbi Didn't Have an Answer

When I was a young boy, perhaps age six or seven, I started wondering what happens to us when we die. Is there a life beyond this one? If so, what's it like? I remember my grandfather dying suddenly when I was around this age and the family was very protective with the grandchildren. Everything was hush, hush. I had questions, but no one would talk about it. I was not allowed to attend the funeral.

No one talked about the afterlife in our synagogue. Not the rabbis, not my teachers. It seemed to be a subject everyone avoided.

At age 12, I really wanted this question answered, so I decided to ask the rabbi. He was our spiritual leader. I figured that if anyone would know about such things, he would. So I made an appointment to talk to him.

He was a busy man, but he was patient and gracious with me, which helped to put me at ease. I got straight to the point.

"Rabbi, what happens to us when we die? Do we go to heaven?"

He smiled and nodded.

"Imagine you're climbing a mountain," he said. "Up ahead you can see a huge forest of trees. There are boulders in your way. You can't really see what's at the top of the mountain or what is over it on the other side."

I wasn't sure where he was going, so I just kept listening intently.

"That's the way it is in life," he explained. "We're all climbing up the mountain. God alone is on top of the mountain and sees what lies beyond. Only He knows what we'll find on the other side."

It wasn't the answer I wanted. In fact, it wasn't much of an answer at all, and I left his office feeling more confused than when I'd gone in. It wasn't until years later that I actually figured it out. The rabbi couldn't tell me whether there was life after death because he didn't know...but he was the rabbi and he couldn't just say, "I have no idea!"

Sadly, this is a familiar position for many Jews.

In ancient Israel, the two main schools of thought consisted of the Pharisees and the Sadducees. We might consider them to be the top two political parties of their day, and Yeshua had many run-ins with members of both parties. The Pharisees often tried to trip Him up on matters of the law, whereas the Sadducees asked a number of "tricky" questions about life after death, which Yeshua usually answered with rhetorical questions.

According to the first-century Jewish historian Josephus, the Pharisees said:

> Souls have an immortal vigor in them.... Under the earth there will be rewards and punishments according as they have lived virtuously or viciously in this life.... The latter are to be detained in an everlasting prison.... The former shall have power to revive and live again.[3]

Another source concludes:

> The Pharisees...maintained that an after-life existed and that God punished the wicked and rewarded the righteous in the world to come. They also believed in a messiah who would herald an era of world peace.... The Sadducees were elitists who wanted to maintain the priestly caste, but they were also liberal in their willingness to incorporate Hellenism into their lives, something the Pharisees opposed. The Sadducees rejected the idea of the Oral Law and insisted on a

literal interpretation of the Written Law; consequently, they did not believe in an afterlife, since they did not see any explicit mention of it in the Torah and the references relating to death and the grave were not understandable to them. The main focus of Sadducee life was rituals associated with the Temple. The Sadducees disappeared around 70 A.D., after the destruction of the Second Temple. None of the writings of the Sadducees has survived, so the little we know about them comes from their Pharisaic opponents.[4]

The Sadducees may have disappeared from the scene centuries ago, but their belief—or rather, lack of belief—about the afterlife lives on. Today, many adherents of Reform Judaism (a less traditional form of Jewish faith and practice) would say that the individual soul itself does not survive death. Instead, it is the nation of Israel that survives and continues, even though individuals die and pass into nothingness.

IS DEATH THE END?

Rabbi Richard L. Rubenstein, a member of the Union of American Hebrew Congregations, the umbrella organization for the Reform Movement, spoke for adherents of this branch of Judaism when he wrote:

> Even as a child…I believed that when I died the whole world of my existence would disappear with me. My world would last only as long as I did. I was convinced that I had arisen out of nothingness and was destined to return to nothingness. All human beings

were locked in the same fatality. In the final analysis, omnipotent nothingness was lord of all creation. Even as a rabbi, I have never really departed from my earliest primordial feelings about my place in the cosmos.[5]

Asher Ginsberg, one of the most respected Jewish thinkers of the late 19th and early 20th centuries, wrote, "The individual dies: die he must; all his hopes for the future cannot save him from death. But the nation has a spiritual thread of life, and physical laws do not set a limit to its years or its strength. And so, let it but make the future of an integral part of its self, though it be only in the form of a fanciful hope...."[6]

Now I want to make it clear that a majority of the Jewish people do not agree with the rabbis just quoted or the Sadducees. The most recent research I've seen shows that close to 60 percent of Jews believe in life after death—and the percentage is increasing. That equates to almost two out of three Jews believe in an afterlife.

And *Gates of Prayer*, the prayer book that was officially approved by the Union for Reform Judaism and the Central Conference of American Rabbis, contains prayers like the following:

> O Lord, God of the spirits of all flesh, You are close to the hearts of the sorrowing, to strengthen and console them with the warmth of Your love, and with the assurance that the human spirit is enduring and indestructible (page 646).

> Only this have we been taught, and in this we put our trust: from You comes the spirit and to You it must return (page 548).

The soul that You have given me, O God, is a pure one! You have created and formed it, breathed it into me, and within me You sustain it. So long as I have breath, therefore, I will give thanks to You, O Lord my God and God of all ages, Master of all creation, Lord of every human spirit. Blessed is the Lord, in whose hands are the souls of all the living and the spirits of all flesh (page 53).

It may be true that the Torah doesn't say *explicitly* that life goes on beyond the grave. But as we'll see, there are certainly some veiled references to heaven in the first five books of the Bible.

As a Jew myself, I find it disheartening that so many influential Jews have denied the existence of the soul or the possibility of eternal life. Although the Sadducees disappeared from history long ago, their philosophy continues to influence the thinking of many great Jews.

For example, because *Albert Einstein* said so much about God, some people have mistakenly suggested that he was a believer. But that was not the case. Einstein's "God" was the impersonal force that holds the universe together—some substance of power that was far beyond humankind's comprehension and did not care about human beings. When asked if he believed in immortality, he said, "No, and one life is enough for me."[7]

Sigmund Freud believed that belief in God or eternal life is nothing more than wishful thinking. He said, "It would be nice if there were a God who created the world and was a benevolent providence, and if there were a moral order in the universe and an after-life; but it is a very striking fact that all this is exactly as we are bound to wish for."[8]

Abba Hillel Silver, a rabbi who was instrumental in the founding of the State of Israel, dismissed the book of Daniel's teaching about the resurrection as an idea that had been absorbed from surrounding cultures, an idea "to which the Jews added nothing original."[9]

The great Jewish philosopher *Benedict De Spinoza* believed that part of the mind—the intellect—survives death and becomes part of "God." But he also believed that all emotions, memories, and personal attributes die when the body does—so his philosophy is not at all comforting.

How sad that so many brilliant thinkers came to this conclusion. Many of them never even bothered to read their own Scriptures; or if they did, simply dismissed some important passages that reveal that life does not end at the grave. They began with a presupposition that this life was all there was and interpreted everything they experienced through this paradigm.

The Amidah, "The Standing Prayer," one of the central prayers of the Jewish liturgy, has a beautiful affirmation of life beyond the grave. This prayer is found in the Siddur, the traditional Jewish prayer book. It is to be recited at each of three prayer services in a typical weekday—morning, afternoon, and evening. The prayer contains 18 sections, or blessings. The second blessing, titled *The God of Nature,* says:

> You O Lord, are mighty forever. You revive the dead, you have the power to save. You sustain the living with loving kindness, you revive the dead with great mercy, you support the falling, heal the sick, set free the bond and keep faith with those who sleep in the dust. Who is like you, O doer of mighty acts? Who resembles you, a king who puts to death and restores

to life, and cause salvation to flourish? And you are certain to revive the dead. Blessed are you, O Lord, who revives the dead.

Five times, the prayer says that God revives the dead. It also says that God "restores to life." Countless Jews have prayed this prayer over and over through the centuries, yet many simply seem to ignore the words. Perhaps they just don't care or do not want to give it any thought. For others, it may just be too overwhelming.

On the flipside, many brilliant Jewish thinkers and spiritual leaders have affirmed belief in life after death, including the great 12th century *Rabbi Maimonides*. The Stanford Encyclopedia of Philosophy calls Maimonides, "the greatest Jewish philosopher of the medieval period" and "the leading rabbinic authority of his time and quite possibly of all time."

Maimonides, also known as The Rambam, included 13 principles of faith in his commentary on the Mishnah. The 13th of these states: "I believe with perfect faith that there will be a revival of the dead at the time when it shall please the Creator, Blessed be His Name."[10]

Baal Shem Tov, the founder of Hasidic Judaism, is another famous Jew who believed devoutly in a life beyond this one. Born as Yisroel Ben Eliezer in the Ukraine in 1698, he was orphaned by the age of five, and cared for by others in his community. He was something of a mystic from his earliest years. Reportedly, he was often absent from school, and was usually found somewhere in the hills or forests on the outskirts of town, contemplating the beauty of nature.

He claimed to have had a vision of heaven in which he saw things that were too wonderful to describe. According to legend, on the morning of his death, he called his disciples around him, gave them instructions for his burial, and asked for a prayer book because "I wish to spend some time communing with *Hashem Yitbarach* (the Name, may He be blessed)."

He also told his disciples that the two clocks in the house would stop running as a sign when his soul departed his body. They later reported that everything happened as he said it would, and said they saw his soul leave his body in the form of a blue flame.

My point in repeating this legend isn't to say I believe any of this—but rather to show that it is not true, as some teach, that the Jewish faith has always been nebulous about life after death. Again, many influential Jews have held strong beliefs about the afterlife. In fact, most Jews throughout history have believed in the concept of heaven for the righteous.

Today, many well-known Jews continue to affirm the belief in life after death. Radio personality *Dennis Prager* is one of them. He writes:

> As I have long believed and as logic dictates, if there is a God and that God is just, there is an afterlife. It's really that simple. In fact, it is axiomatic. Given the stupendous injustices of this life, only an afterlife enables justice.
>
> Also, because God is the ultimate incorporeal reality, the physical world cannot be the only realm of existence.
>
> Those Jews who doubt God's existence have every reason to doubt an afterlife. But if you believe in a just God, there is an afterlife.

What is the afterlife? I have no clue and do not spend even five minutes a year meditating on it (except to hope that all those I love are there with me).

However, my belief in God and the afterlife keep me sane. The thought that this life is all there is, that children are burned alive and that's their lousy luck, that their torturers get away with it and that's their good luck, that this life is all one big crapshoot—such beliefs would drive me mad. I don't see how it doesn't drive mad those who deny God and the afterlife and who are sensitive to all the unjust suffering in the world.[11]

My only advice to Dennis is that he should take the time to find out what the Scriptures say concerning our responsibility before a just God. Yes, there is a heaven, but what does God require of us to get in? He should spend well more than five minutes a year meditating on this issue because it is one of the great questions of life—and the Bible has the answers.

Abraham Joshua Heschel, who served as professor of Jewish Ethics and Mysticism at the Jewish Theological Seminary of America, was considered one of the great Jewish theologians of the 20th century. When asked whether Jews believed in life after death, he replied, "I'll give you the real answer, we believe in an afterlife, but we have no information about it." He went on to say, "I think that's God's business what to do with me after life. This, here, it's my business what to do with my life. So, I leave it to Him. I am so busy trying to live a good life, and I don't always succeed, I have no time to worry what God's going to do with me once I'm in the grave. Who knows what He expects of me in the grave?"[12]

Still, Heschel wrote passionately about his belief in the afterlife. In his essay, "Death as Homecoming," he writes:

> Human life is on its way from a great distance; it has gone through ages of experience, of growing, suffering, insight, action. We are what we are by what we come from. There is a vast continuum preceding individual existence, and it is a legitimate surmise to assume that there is a continuum following individual existence. Human living is always being under way, and death is not the final destination.
>
> In the language of the Bible to die, to be buried, is said to be "gathered to his people" (Genesis 25:8). They "were gathered to their fathers" (Judges 2:10). "When your days are fulfilled to go to be with your fathers" (I Chronicles 17:11).
>
> Do souls become dust? Does spirit turn to ashes? How can souls, capable of creating immortal words, immortal works of thought and art, be completely dissolved, vanish forever?
>
> Others may counter: The belief that man may have a share in eternal life is not only beyond proof; it is even presumptuous. Who could seriously maintain that members of the human species, a class of mammals, will attain eternity? What image of humanity is presupposed by the belief in immortality? Indeed, man's hope for eternal life presupposes that there is something about man that is worthy of eternity, that

has some affinity to what is divine, that is made in the likeness of the divine....[13]

Yitz (Irving) Greenberg is an influential Orthodox rabbi, scholar, and author. He served as president of Jewish Life Network/Steinhardt Foundation and as funding president of the National Jewish Center for Learning and Leadership. He says, "Belief in the afterlife—a world to come in which the righteous get their true reward and the wicked get their deserved comeuppance—is a central teaching of traditional Judaism."[14]

HEAVEN IN THE SCRIPTURES

Furthermore, some ancient rabbis saw clear evidence for the hereafter in the Torah. San Hedrin 91b says: "Rabbi Meir said: Where can we see that resurrection is derived from the Torah? In the passage: 'Then will Moses and the children of Israel sing this song to the Lord' (Exodus 15:1). It does not say 'sang' (past tense) but *'will* sing' (future). Therefore, resurrection is deductible from the Torah. Again, Rabbi Joshua B. Levi asked, Where can we see that resurrection is derived from the Torah? In the passage 'Happy are those who dwell in Your house, they will be still praising you' (Psalms 84:5), it is not stated, 'they have praised You' but *'will be* praising You' [in the hereafter]; therefore resurrection is derived from the Torah (Psalms)."[15]

There are a number of other Scriptures throughout the Tanakh that seem to make veiled references to the righteous dead being in heaven with their loved ones. For example, Genesis 25:8 says that after Abraham died, he was "gathered to his people." The same thing is said about Ishmael (Genesis 25:17), Isaac (35:29), and Jacob (49:33).

Some commentators have claimed that this is a reference to being buried in a family burial plot. But that doesn't make sense for two reasons. First, regarding the death of Jacob, the Bible says, "When Jacob had finished giving instructions to his sons, he drew his feet up into the bed, breathed his last and was gathered to his people." In the next chapter, we find that the Egyptian physicians took 40 days to embalm Jacob. After that, Joseph carried his father's body back to the land of Canaan to bury him there. In other words, Jacob was "gathered to his people" long before he was buried.

Then in Deuteronomy 32:50, we find God saying to Moses, "There on the mountain that you have climbed you will die and be gathered to your people..." But two chapters later, we read, "And Moses the servant of the Lord died there in Moab, as the Lord had said. He buried him in Moab, in the valley opposite Beth Peor, but to this day no one knows where his grave is" (Deuteronomy 34:5-6). So again, Moses being "gathered to his people" couldn't possibly have anything to do with where he was buried.

The whole concept takes on new significance when we turn to the New Testament and read the parable of the rich man and Lazarus. In this parable, related to the disciples by Yeshua Himself, when Lazarus, the poor man, died, "the angels carried him to *Abraham's side* [or Abraham's bosom]." It is clear here that the beggar was alive and present with Abraham and his ancestors. He had been "gathered to his people."[16]

That the reality of a literal heaven is revealed in the Old Testament and was embraced and declared by the ancient leaders of Israel is further supported in the book of 1 Kings. In chapter 8 we find King Solomon standing before the altar of the temple "in front of the whole assembly," spreading forth his hands to heaven. Then he prayed:

> *Lord, the God of Israel, there is no God like you in heaven above or on earth below—you who keep your covenant of love with your servants who continue whole-heartedly in your way. ...But will God really dwell on earth? The heavens, even the highest heaven, cannot contain you. How much less this temple I have built! Yet give attention to your servant's prayer and his plea for mercy, Lord my God. Hear the cry and the prayer that your servant is praying in your presence this day. May your eyes be open toward this temple night and day, this place of which you said, "My Name shall be there," so that you will hear the prayer your servant prays toward this place. Hear the supplication of your servant and of your people Israel when they pray toward this place. Hear from heaven, your dwelling place, and when you hear, forgive* (1 Kings 8:22,27-30 NIV).

An entire, fully formed theology of heaven is encapsulated in this passage. Solomon speaks of a dwelling place of God, from which He sees all and judges all. Clearly, ancient Jewish thought had conceived of such a place from earliest times. The proof is in Scripture.

The account of the prophet Elijah in 2 Kings is yet another illuminating example:

> *When the Lord was about to take Elijah up to heaven in a whirlwind, Elijah and Elisha were on their way from Gilgal. ...As they were walking along and talking together, suddenly a chariot of fire and horses of fire*

appeared and separated the two of them, and Elijah
went up to heaven in a whirlwind. Elisha saw this
and cried out, "My father! My father! The chariots and
horsemen of Israel!" And Elisha saw him no more..."
(2 Kings 2:1,11-12 NIV).

Yet again, the conclusion is clear: Elijah, a righteous man in the
eyes of the Lord, was taken into heaven, the abode of the righteous,
there to receive his reward.

And when we get to the book of Daniel, we find what may be
the clearest revelation about the afterlife in the entire Tanakh:

Multitudes who sleep in the dust of the earth will awake:
some to everlasting life, others to shame and everlasting
contempt. Those who are wise will shine like the bright-
ness of the heavens, and those who lead many to righ-
teousness, like the stars for ever and ever (Daniel 12:2-3
NIV).

Anyone who reads these Scriptures with an open mind should
conclude that there is life after death. In fact, these verses in Daniel
actually illuminate for us the reality of both a heaven and hell. Those
who "sleep in the dust of the earth" refers those who have died. To
awake speaks of some kind of resurrection or second life. He states
that some will awake to "everlasting life" which I believe is referring
to heaven, while others to "shame and everlasting contempt." This
description sounds a lot like hell to me, but more on that later. Keep
in mind, Daniel is part of the Old Testament (Tanakh), not the New
Testament. These verses should dispel the myth once and for all that
the Old Testament does not mention an afterlife.

Heaven in the Apocryphal Writings

From about 200 years before the birth of Yeshua until 200 years after, Jewish writers produced a number of apocryphal books such as the Testament of Benjamin, First and Second Maccabees, and the various books of Enoch and Esdras. These books are not accepted as Scripture, but they are considered to be important historical documents, and they reflect Jewish thinking of their times. Although many prominent teachers and rabbis today focus more on the survival of the Jewish people and this takes precedence over any thought of individual immortality, the historic writings of the Apocrypha place a greater emphasis on the survival of the human soul.

For example, the book of Enoch, which is referred to in the New Testament book of Jude (verse 14), insists that the soul and body are not the same thing—that the soul can and does survive even as the body decays.[17]

In the seventh chapter of the book of 4 Ezra, we read:

> *When the decisive decree has gone forth from the Most High that a man will die, as the spirit leaves the body to return again to him who gave it, first of all it adores the glory of the Most High. And if is one of those who have shown scorn and who have not kept the way of the Most High, and have despised His law, and have hated those who fear God—such spirits shall not enter into habitations, but shall immediately wander about in torments, ever grieving and sad in seven ways...*
> (4 Ezra 7:78-81).

The book of Jubilees, dated to about 200 B.C., also speaks of the resurrection of the dead:

And then the Lord will heal his servants, and they will rise up and see great peace. And they will drive out their enemies, and the righteous ones will see and give praise and rejoice forever and ever with joy...they will know that the Lord is an executor of judgment; and he will show mercy to hundreds and thousands, to all who love him (Jubilees 23:30-31).

Authors Rifat Sonsino and Daniel B. Syme confirm that many rabbis throughout the Middle Ages believed that the human soul is separate from the body:

The idea of the soul's separation from the body after death was affirmed by many rabbis throughout the Middle Ages and beyond. Saadia ben Yosef al Fayummi concurred with the view that every person is endowed with a soul. He added, however, that this soul is created by God at the time when the human body is completed, and thus does not have a preexisting life. After death, the soul leaves for the world to come until resurrection when, together with the body, it will undergo a final judgment. Isaac Israeli (ca. 850–950) and Judah Yalevi (born about 1080) advanced similar opinions. Yet there were other Jewish thinkers, particularly those influenced by Greek philosophy, who believed that the soul, but not the body, was immortal and the soul would live but the body would decay.[18]

THE WORLD TO COME

Ancient Jewish writings also contain many references to *Olam Haba*, the World to Come, or a "New Earth." While the Torah itself speaks only briefly of this concept, there is a rich tradition of exposition and explanation in rabbinic teaching. Olam Haba consists primarily of two crucial concepts. The first is that man's immortal soul will return to its Creator after death. Closely following on this is a belief in the resurrection of the dead at the end of time. The ancient rabbis taught that the soul of man departs the body at the moment of death but returns to it at the time of resurrection.

The rabbis also taught that man's deeds, good and bad, are rewarded and punished not here on earth, but in the afterlife. It is an idea articulated in the Mishnah, where many references can be found regarding the World to Come. According to Rabbi Yaakov, for example, "This world is like a lobby before the World to Come; prepare yourself in the lobby so that you can enter the banquet hall."[19]

Similarly, the Tractate Moed Katan teaches, "This world is only like a hotel. The world to come is like a home."[20]

Although many rabbis seemed to think of the world to come as a supernatural renovation of the earth that would take place at the end of time, not everyone saw it that way. The Midrash says:

> *The sages have taught us that we human beings cannot appreciate they joys of the future age. Therefore they called it "the coming world" [Olam Ha-Ba] not because it does not yet exist, but because it is still in the future. "The world to come" is the one waiting for man after this world. But there is no basis for the assumption that the world to come will only begin after the destruction*

of this world. What it does imply is that when the righteous leave this world, they ascend on high, as it is said: "How great is the goodness, O Lord, which you have in store for those who fear you, and which, toward those who take refuge in you, you show in the sight of men." (Psalm 31:20)[21]

One of the most vivid descriptions of paradise came from Immanuel ben Solomon of Rome:

> Tables and candlesticks, thrones and crowns were there to be seen; they were for the souls that were pure and clean; and here was a throne of ivory, great in size, overlaid with gold in wealth, giving life unto those who reached it, and unto their flesh giving health; and the stones of a crown shone forth upon it on high; while garments of blue and purple and scarlet were spread, and about it did lay like polished copper gleaming, unto all lands their beauty beaming.[22]

Authors Sonsino and Syme write:

> It was generally accepted that in the world to come (haolam haba), the righteous would be rewarded and the wicked punished. The rabbis taught that the former would go to Paradise (in Hebrew, Gan Eden, the Garden of Eden) and the latter to Hell (in Hebrew gehinnom, Gehenna). Beyond these basic tenets, however, individual rabbis offered imaginative scenarios. Some sages argued that the righteous and the wicked would go to their respective places only after resurrection and final judgment. Others maintained that the

departed would assume their assigned locations immediately following death.[23]

Other rabbis agree that the righteous person who dies will
receive his or her reward immediately, instead of waiting for the
resurrection and the creation of a new earth. According to Midrash
Pesikta Rabbati, "When a man is righteous, his righteousness is
recorded; when a man does wrong, his wrongdoing is recorded.
Accordingly, when a righteous man arrives at the end of his days,
his recording angels precede him into Heaven singing his praise…
But when a wicked man dies, a man who did not bring himself to
turn in repentance to God, the Holy Blessed One, says to him, 'Let
your soul be blasted in despair. How many times did I call upon
you to repent and you did not?'"[24]

The same tractate says, "The elder R. Hiyya said: 'When a holy
man leaves this world, three companies of angels attend him, one
saying, "Let him come in peace," (Isaiah 57:2): another saying, "Let
him rest in his bed," (Isaiah 57:2): and another walking before him
in silence….'"[25]

OTHER EARLY JEWISH VIEWS OF HEAVEN

The precedent for a belief in a heavenly realm reaches back to
the earliest roots of Judaism. In the Tanakh, heaven is referred to as
shamayim and is located above a solid, transparent dome that covers
the earth. It was here that Yahweh dwelt, just as His dwelling place
on earth was Solomon's temple in Jerusalem. The temple, in fact, was
constructed as a model of the cosmos and included a sacred precinct
that represented heaven.

Jewish Kabbalah mysticism speaks of seven separate levels of heaven. (Please understand that I do not agree with nor am I endorsing Kabbalah teachings. I am presenting this as some of the thinking that has taken place within the broader context of Judaism.)

The first level of heaven was the aforementioned *shamayim,* which according to the Kabbalistic mystics, was ruled by the Archangel Gabriel and was considered the abode of Adam and Eve. The second level was *raqia,* the heaven that Moses supposedly visited and where he beheld "a retinue of fifty myriads of angels all fashioned out of fire and water." It was here, also, where the fallen angels were imprisoned after Lucifer rebelled against God.

Shehaqim was the name of the third heaven. It served as the home for the Garden of Eden and the Tree of Life. *Ma'on,* the fourth level, was ruled by the Archangel Michael. According to Talmud Hagiga 12, it is the location also of heavenly Jerusalem, the temple, and the altar.

After *makhon* and *zebul,* the fifth and six heavens, respectively, comes the supreme, or seventh heaven, the holiest of all the levels in the Kabbalistic scheme. Known as *araboth,* this holiest height of heaven houses the throne of glory and is attended by seven archangels. Underneath the throne, according to the Kabbalah, lies the abode of all unborn human souls as well as the home of the seraphim and cherubim.

Admittedly, these writings are extremely mystical, complex, and esoteric, but they illustrate that the concept of heaven is very real in Judaism and is prevalent in many Jewish sacred texts.

REINCARNATION AND THE JEWS

You may be surprised to learn that many ultra-orthodox Jews also believe in reincarnation—although their version of reincarnation differs from that taught by Far Eastern religions in one significant way. Jewish reincarnationists generally teach that the soul has *chosen* to return to earth to finish some task that was left undone, or to be further purified. They do not believe that the person who has behaved badly in life will be punished by being reborn into poverty or a lower state of existence.

Reincarnation is likely a rather late entry into the Jewish belief system, although a number of fairly ancient texts do focus on the subject. The first of these is the *Zohar,* the foundational text of Kabbalah, which first appeared in Spain in the 1200s.

The Zohar was published by a writer named Moses de Leon, but he claimed that the book was originally written by Shimon bar Yochai, a legendary rabbi of the second century. Legend had it that bar Yochai spent 13 years in a cave hiding from the Romans and studying the Torah, and de Leon claimed he had written the Zohar in that cave after being inspired by the prophet Elijah. Modern scholarship disputes that claim.

Other old texts that refer to reincarnation include *Shaar HaGilgulim,* which comes from the 16th century, and *Nishmat Hayyim,* written by Rabbi Manasseh ben Israel, who lived in the 1660s. He wrote:

> The belief or the doctrine of the transmigration of souls is a firm and infallible dogma accepted by the whole assemblage of our church with one accord, so there is none to be found who would dare to deny it…. Indeed, there is a great number of sages in Israel who hold firm to this doctrine so that they made it a dogma, a fundamental point of our religion. We are therefore duty bound to obey and to accept this dogma with

acclamation...as the truth of it has been incontestably demonstrated by the Zohar and the Kabbalists.

Kabbalists teach that the soul is a divine spark of the eternal. It exists in heaven before it chooses to enter into a human body because there is something it can accomplish here on earth that cannot be done in the heavenly realm. They say the soul also lives on after that body has died. That's fairly easy to understand. But now it gets complicated.

They also teach that the soul is made up of 613 channels, which parallel the 248 limbs and 365 blood vessels of the body. These 613 channels attain eternal salvation when all 613 *Mitzvot*—or commands of the Jewish law—have been fulfilled. They believe that when a person dies, the part of the soul that was purified by studying the Torah and performing Mitzvot goes on to Gan Eden, or paradise. It is only the non-perfected part of the soul that returns to earth.

They further believe that the first man, Adam, was composed of all future souls. The soul of Jacob was comprised of 70 parts, which were then further subdivided into the 600,000 souls of Israel. These 600,000 were then subdivided further and so on and so on, until you reach the seven billion people who live in the world today.

Do I believe any of this? Of course not. Hebrews 9:27 says that people are destined to die once and, after that, face judgment. That's pretty clear. Dying once doesn't leave much room for reincarnation. Or any room, actually.

Who May Enter Paradise?

Over the centuries, the great Jewish sages have not agreed over who will and who will not be admitted to this paradise. Some insisted that paradise was open only to the children of Israel, but this seems to have never been the prevailing view. In the second century, Rabbi Joshua ben Hananiah pronounced, "Righteous gentiles have a place in the world to come."[26]

Centuries later, the philosopher Maimonides stated, "The pious of all nations of the world have a portion in the world to come."[27] In his commentary on the Mishnah, he added, "The resurrection of the dead is one of the cardinal principles established by Moses our Teacher. A person who does not believe in this principle has no real religion, certainly not Judaism. However, resurrection is only for the righteous."[28]

The resurrection of the dead became one of the fundamental beliefs in Rabbinic Judaism, although the rabbis disagreed over how and when it would happen. Rabbi Hiyya ben Joseph taught that "the dead will come up through the ground and rise up in Jerusalem...and the righteous will rise up fully clothed."[29]

Writing in the 10th century, Saadia ben Yosef al-Fayyumi (892-942 CE), the head of the academy of Sura, wrote:

> Even fire, which causes things to be burned so quickly, merely effects the separation of the parts of a thing... causing the dust part to return to ashes.... It does not however, bring about the annihilation of anything. Nor is it conceivable that anyone should have the power to annihilate anything to the point where it would vanish

completely except its Creator, who produced it out of nothing.

Since then the matter can be thus explained, in view of the fact that none of the constituent parts of the human being who has been devoured could have been annihilated, they must all have been set aside, wheresoever they may have taken up, whether it be on land or sea, until such time as they are restored in their entirety. Nor would such restoration be any more remarkable than their original creation.[30]

The rabbis also disagreed over the nature of the afterlife. Some believed that the souls of the departed were asleep, awaiting the day when they would be reunited with their resurrected physical bodies. Others denied that there would be a resurrection of the physical body, but used the term "resurrection" to mean that the soul would live on after the death of the body. Either way, the soul, the internal essence of the human being, the spark of the divine within, would live on beyond the grave.

As Maimonides wrote in his *Guide to the Perplexed,* "Soul (nefesh)…is also a term denoting the rational soul, I mean the form of man…. And it is a term denoting the thing that remains of man after death."

In his book *Jewish Views of the Afterlife,* Simcha Paull Raphael says:

Within both Talmud and Midrash are found vast collections of theology on immortality and the afterlife journey of the soul. The teachings are based on the conceptions of the afterlife found in the Hebrew Bible and apocalyptic literature. But Rabbinic postmortem teaching frequently move in a new direction and have a character of their own, building on the past, but reflecting the unique spiritual worldview of the Rabbis.

As in biblical and apocryphal writings, nowhere in Rabbinic literature do we find a single, systemized statement on the Jewish understanding of life after death. There is certainly no such thing as a Talmudic tractate on the hereafter.... What we find instead are thousands of individual Rabbinic teachings on various facets of death and the hereafter randomly dispersed throughout Talmudic and Midrashic literature.[31]

He adds that "...many distinct and disparate notions of the afterlife coexist, some related to collective resurrection of the dead, others to individual immortality."

ETERNITY IN THE GARDEN OF EDEN

Another Jewish term for heaven is "Gan Eden," which is Hebrew for Garden of Eden. As I'm sure you already know, this garden is first mentioned in the book of Genesis. It is where Adam and Eve were placed after they were created, and it is where we are told they committed the first sin by eating fruit from the Tree of Knowledge of Good and Evil. After this, God cast them out of the garden (Genesis 3:23-24).

The Bible even gives a fairly good description of the location of Gan Eden.

> A river watering the garden flowed from Eden; from there it was separated into four headwaters. The name of the first is the Pishon; it winds through the entire

land of Havilah, where there is gold. (The gold of that land is good; aromatic resin and onyx are also there.) The name of the second river is the Gihon; it winds through the entire land of Cush. The name of the third river is the Tigris: it runs along the east side of Ashur. And the fourth river is the Euphrates (Genesis 2:10-14 NIV).

Later in Jewish thought, Gan Eden came to be thought of as a place where the souls of the righteous go after death. Some rabbis seemed to believe this would happen in the distant future, at the time of the resurrection. Exodus Rabbah 15:7 says, "In the Messianic Age, God will establish peace for [the nations] and they will sit at ease and eat in Gan Eden." It's not clear whether the nations are the righteous dead or people who happen to be living during the distant Messianic Age.

But there are other texts that clearly describe Gan Eden as an immediate destination for the righteous dead. In Barakhot 28b, we find the story of Rabbi Yohanan ben Zakkai on his deathbed. Just before he dies, ben Zakki says, "There are two roads before me, one leading to Gan Eden and the other to Gehenna, and I do not know by which I shall be taken."

Later Jewish texts describe Gan Eden in great detail. Yalkut Shimoni Bereshit 20 speaks of "gates of ruby, by which stand sixty myriads and ministering angels." The Tree of Life stands in the center of the garden and contains "five hundred thousand varieties of fruit all differing in appearance and taste."

The Maggid of Mezhirich says that a person's kind deeds are used by God as seeds for the planting of trees in Gan Eden; thus each man creates his own paradise. The reverse is true when he transgresses the law.

Rabbi Yakov Yosef of Polnoi taught that no Gehenna could be worse for the wicked than Gan Eden. After all, the biggest pleasure there will be is joy from the presence of the Lord. Since the wicked didn't train themselves for it in this world, they can never appreciate it in the next world.

Before we leave our discussion of the Jewish view of heaven, let's take a look at some thoughts from a few Jewish leaders of the modern era. I'll begin with Dr. Alvin J. Reines, professor of Jewish Philosophy at the Hebrew Union College-Jewish Institute of Religion in Cincinnati:

> My position is finitism. I do not believe there is a personal after existence. When I die, my individual identity will be annihilated, and both my psyche and body will perish... The only position for which I have credible evidence is that death brings an end to the psychic and physical existence of a human being...In my view...divine power is limited to the point where God is incapable of being the ground (cause) of any kind of existence other than finite beings. It is not, therefore, humans alone who are finite, but everything that exists is necessarily finite, from subatomic particles to galaxies and the universe itself. Accordingly, human death is not the result of divine punishment, but the result of divine finity.[32]

Rabbi Alexander M. Schindler served as president of the Union of American Hebrew Congregations and as president of the Conference of Presidents of Major American Jewish Organizations. He wrote:

The death of my beloved father in 1957, in conjunction with my work as a rabbi in homes made sad and still by death, marked an awakening for me to the intuition that death was a portal rather than a sealed wall... Many men and women who I encountered shared and reinforced that faith. They were every bit as modern and as "enlightened" as I saw myself to be. There was Jimmy Heller, for instance. He was the rabbi of one of the largest Reform Congregations in our land, a well-educated, brilliant Renaissance man. He was a leader of Labor Zionism. He wrote the program notes for the Cincinnati symphony. He was a ranking bridge player. His writings and preachings were soulful and intellectually powerful. And he believed with full faith in immortality in the deathlessness of the souls—of each individual soul, with a full awareness of its particular past and being... I remember visiting Rabbi Heller on his deathbed. He was radiant with confidence. He did not regret his imminent passing. He saw it as precisely that, a "passing" from this world to another—to a world where he could once again embrace his father.... I left his bedside with a sense that I would miss him rather than mourn him; I would feel his absence as one feels the absence of a traveler.[33]

Writing in *The American Rabbi,* Bernard S. Raskas gave "A Jewish View of Immortality":

What is this immortality in which I believe?

I believe that a person lives on in his or her family....

I believe there is a form of immortality in the institutions we build and the causes we espouse....

I believe in the immortality of friendship and helpfulness....

I believe in the immortality of existence....

I find immortality in my people....

Rabbi Raskas continues:

I was with my people when they were part of the exodus from Egypt. I stood with them at Mount Sinai to receive the Ten Commandments. The pronouncements of Isaiah pound in my blood. The sayings of Akiba are sealed in the cells of my brain. The message of Maimonides is part of my mind. I experienced the Holocaust and shared in the agony of my people. I participated in the birth of modern Israel and the ecstasy of my people. I say this, not in arrogance, but in awesome humility. As a member of the Jewish people, I am immortal.[34]

Beautiful words, to be sure. But not very comforting to one who has lost a loved one, or who has come face to face with his own mortality. We can see from these three examples some of the variety of views that exist among the Jewish people and their leaders. There is no consensus on life after death or the matter of heaven.

Some claim that heaven is a Christian invention. We've seen that this is clearly not the case. Hundreds of cultures from all periods of history have believed in a paradise where the righteous dead will be rewarded. Ecclesiastes says that God has set eternity in the human heart. This has been my experience since childhood, and I see the same in thousands and thousands I have ministered to over the years in dozens of nations. We've seen that this is clearly true. We've also seen that the concept of heaven has been a significant topic of Jewish belief and teaching for centuries. But what about Christians? What does Christianity teach historically? What do we learn about heaven in the New Testament, and how does this differ from Judaism and the Old Testament?

Chapter 5

THE CHRISTIAN VIEW OF HEAVEN

ASK 100 CHRISTIANS WHAT heaven will be like, and you'll probably get 100 different responses. A random sampling:

"Heaven is a place where everyone is happy."

"It's where I'll be reunited with my loved ones who have died."

"There won't be any stress there."

"In heaven, we'll all worship God forever."

"The weather will be perfect, we'll all have everything we could possibly want, and the food will be, well...to die for."

Although Christians have many different ideas about heaven, there are some themes that come up again and again:

- Heaven is a real place.

- It is where redeemed souls will live forever in God's presence.

- Those who go to heaven will experience never-ending joy.

- There will be no sickness, crime, hunger, poverty, terrorism, war, or any other bad thing in heaven.

- God will wipe all tears from our eyes and we will be able to forget all about any pain and suffering we might have experienced in this life.

EARLY CHRISTIAN VIEWS OF HEAVEN

The early Christians didn't talk much about heaven during the first years after Jesus' death and resurrection. The reason for this was that they expected their Messiah to return almost immediately to set up an eternal kingdom here on earth. In other words, they didn't think much about heaven because they didn't expect to die.

But as time passed, and Yeshua's followers began to pass into eternity—many of them executed in gruesome ways by the Romans—thoughts naturally turned to the afterlife. Where had the departed believers gone? Were they asleep, awaiting the resurrection, or were they in paradise? The latter seemed likely, especially given the parable of Lazarus and the Rich Man, and keeping in mind what Jesus had promised the repentant thief on the cross next to Him, "I tell you, today you shall be with Me in Paradise" (Luke 23:43).

And then too, just prior to His crucifixion, Jesus had told His apostles:

> Do not let your heart be troubled. Trust in God; trust also in Me. In My Father's house are many dwelling places. If it were not so, would I have told you that I

am going to prepare a place for you? If I go and prepare
a place for you, I will come back again and take you
to Myself, so that where I am you may also be (John
14:1-3).

Yeshua also told His disciples, "In the world you will have trouble, but take heart! I have overcome the world!" (John 16:33). And He told Pontius Pilate, "My kingdom is not of this world. If My kingdom were of this world, then My servants would be fighting so that I wouldn't be handed over to the Judean leaders. But as it is, My kingdom is not from here" (John 18:36).

It seems clear that Jesus is referring to heaven. But even so, there was no clear teaching on the afterlife. Because Christianity sprang out of Judaism, the early church's views about heaven corresponded with Jewish teaching. For example, early Christians fervently believed in and hoped for the resurrection of the dead.

Yeshua Himself was seen as the first of the righteous who would be raised to life at the last days. One often-debated question was, what happened to believers in the time between when they died and were resurrected? Another was whether the eternal life that Jesus gave was meant for the soul or the body. As in Judaism, some of Yeshua's followers believed that the soul and body were inseparable. There was no life without the body. Others argued that all flesh was corrupted by sin, and therefore could not possibly enter paradise. Obviously, they argued, it was only when the soul was freed from the flesh of the body that it could gain entrance into heaven.

In A.D. 95, Clement of Rome declared that Peter and Paul went directly to "the holy place" when they died.[1] But writing a few decades later, Justin Martyr said that the souls of men would not enter heaven—however heaven may be viewed—until the time of the resurrection. He argued against those who believed that only the soul entered heaven:

> And there are some who maintain that even Jesus Himself appeared only as spiritual, and not in flesh, but presented merely the appearance of flesh: these persons seek to rob the flesh of the promise. First, then, let us solve those things which seem to them to be insoluble; then we will introduce in an orderly manner the demonstration concerning the flesh, proving that it partakes of salvation.[2]

Origen, who lived from 185 to 154, wrote in his book *First Principles:*

> I think, therefore, that all the saints who depart from this life will remain in some place situated on the earth, which holy Scripture calls paradise, as in some place of instruction, and, so to speak, class-room or school of souls, in which they are to be instructed regarding all the things which they had seen on earth, and are to receive also some information respecting things that are to follow in the future, as even when in this life they had obtained in some degree indications of future events, although "through a glass darkly," all of which are revealed more clearly and distinctly to the saints in their proper time and place. If anyone indeed be pure in heart, and holy in mind, and more practiced in perception, he will, by making more rapid progress, quickly ascend to a place in the air, and reach the kingdom of heaven, through those

mansions, so to speak, in the various places which the Greeks have termed spheres, i.e., globes, but which holy Scripture has called heavens; in each of which he will first see clearly what is done there, and in the second place, will discover the reason why things are so done: and thus he will in order pass through all gradations, following Him who hath passed into the heavens, Jesus the Son of God, who said, "I will that where I am, these may be also." And of this diversity of places He speaks, when He says, "In My Father's house are many mansions." He Himself is everywhere, and passes swiftly through all things; nor are we any longer to understand Him as existing in those narrow Limits in which He was once confined for our sakes, i.e., not in that circumscribed body which He occupied on earth, when dwelling among men, according to which He might be considered as enclosed in some one place.[3]

Iranaeus, who lived in the second century, believed in the resurrection of the body, but he also taught that the spirits of the saved would live in heaven with God forever. He wrote:

All the blessed in Heaven will see Christ, the glory of the communion of the saints, and the glory of communion and the renovation of the world. They will dwell in their true home, where with Christ they enjoy eternal peace and comfort. Paradise, the heavenly city, the celestial abode, and the reign of God, come together at the endtime, when the Word of God restores the cosmos to himself.[4]

Tertullian, who also lived in the second century, used the term *refrigerium* to refer to the everlasting happiness of heaven, but he taught that only martyrs went there directly upon their deaths. Refrigerium interim was used to denote the interim state, where the souls of those who had not been martyred awaited their final judgment.

In their book *Heaven: A History*, Collen McDannell and Bernhard Lang write:

> The early Christian image of eternal life was distinctive and different from both that of the Pharisees and the Essenes. The chief architect of the new image of Heaven was of course Jesus, but important expansions and modifications were made by Paul and the author of the book of Revelation. In all three cases, Jewish philosophical and metaphysical arguments for an afterlife held less importance than the experience of the divine which promised everlasting blessedness. While earlier writers saw life after death in terms of the re-establishment of the Jewish state or as a special reward for the virtuous, the New Testament Heaven eliminated the notion of compensation. Heaven was not the place or time when an elect group who lacked something would find fulfillment, but rather the promise that Christians would be able to experience the divine fully. Caught up in religious excitement and enthusiasm, followers of Jesus rejected the world and focused their eyes on a future with God alone.[5]

The authors add, "Like contemporary Jewish philosophers, Jesus was not concerned about the fate of dead bodies. What survived after death had spiritual qualities and could be termed a soul. The intense experience which Jesus felt toward the divine would be duplicated in the next life. Earthly concerns of sexuality, family or compensation for lost wealth would be of no importance."[6]

Heaven became more clearly defined in the Christian mind in the early years of the third century, when a book called *The Martyrdom* was widely circulated. It told stories of many who had been martyred for their faith. Among them were two women named Perpetua and Felicity, who had been thrown to wild beasts in Carthage in North Africa. Before her death, Perpetua wrote down a dream she had in prison. In the dream, she went to a beautiful garden where she saw her sickly brother, Dinocrates, who had died at the age of seven. Now he was strong and healthy, and drinking from the fountain of life.[7]

Some believed that paradise had already come to earth and was spreading across the globe. Another father of the early church, Eusebius, who lived from 265 to 340, wrote that "the end" had already come:

> I need now only say, all these things have been done: the old and elementary system passed away with a great noise; all these predicted empires have actually fallen, and the new kingdom, the new heaven and earth, the new Jerusalem—all of which were to descend from God, to be formed by His power, have been realized on earth; all these things have been done in the sight of all the nations; God's holy arm has been made bare in their sight: His judgments have prevailed, and they remain for an everlasting testimony to the whole world, His kingdom has

come, as it was foretold it should, and His will has,
so far, been done.[8]

Chris Armstrong writes, "By the year 400, with the era of
persecution ended, the communal and sensual aspects of heaven
seemed to recede as God himself took center stage again. Christian
leaders wrote increasingly of heaven as, above all, the place where
one participated in God's spiritual perfection. For the 4th-century
Eastern Father Gregory of Nazianzus, Heaven was where the tired
pilgrim could finally rest in God. There the Christian could at last,
released from the distractions of the flesh, enjoy the full nearness of
Christ—tasted only briefly and tantalizingly on earth."[9]

In the same century, Augustine of Hippo wrote his classic work
about heaven, *City of God*. As the Roman Empire tottered on the
edge of collapse, Augustine wrote of a glorious kingdom of joy and
peace that would last forever:

> Alienated from everything pertaining to "this world,"
> ascetic Christians such as Augustine espoused the
> dualistic philosophies of Gnosticism or Neoplatonism.
> They rejected the compensational heaven of Iranaeus
> and predicted that life after death would entail the
> continuation of their ascetic, spiritual lifestyle. As
> spirit was superior to matter on earth, so it would be
> in heaven.[10]

Augustine wrote that in the eternal city of heaven, "the hearts
of all will be transparent, manifest, luminous in the perfection
of love." Gone will be suspicion and confusion. There will be no
darkness, no obscurity in heaven, and hence no division among
its citizens. God's light will shine up the hidden, and in that light,

each to each will be "the better known, the better beloved. ... The universalized love of heaven permits no exclusive, restricted circle of friends. In the heavenly community, friendship will be replaced by love."[11]

THE NEW TESTAMENT ON HEAVEN

Upon reading the New Testament, it becomes apparent that the topic of heaven is addressed with greater frequency and much greater clarity than in the Old Testament. For example, the book of Revelation describes heaven as a place with streets made out of paved gold and surrounded by gates made of precious gems:

> *The wall was made of jasper, and the city of pure gold, as pure as glass. The foundations of the city walls were decorated with every kind of precious stone. The first foundation was jasper, the second sapphire, the third agate, the fourth emerald, the fifth onyx, the sixth ruby, the seventh chrysolite, the eighth beryl, the ninth topaz, the tenth turquoise, the eleventh jacinth, and the twelfth amethyst. The twelve gates were twelve pearls, each gate made of a single pearl. The great street of the city was of gold, as pure as transparent glass. I did not see a temple in the city, because the Lord God Almighty and the Lamb are its temple. The city does not need the sun or the moon to shine on it, for the glory of God gives it light, and the Lamb is its lamp* (Revelation 21:18-23 NIV).

Some people accept this as a literal description. Others see it as the apostle John's way of trying to describe the indescribable.

Either way, by this description, heaven will be a glorious and sublime experience.

Most significant perhaps is that in heaven we will encounter the very presence of our Creator and His Messiah, the Lamb of God (one of the many titles in the Bible for Yeshua, Jesus). He is the one who, through His sacrificial death, has made it possible for us to enter heaven.

Perhaps this is the single most important doctrine of the New Testament—that there is only one way to get into heaven and that way is by believing in Yeshua and His atoning death.

The idea that humanity has been separated from God by sin is established clearly in both the Old and New Testaments. It is this condition of sin and separation that makes us ineligible to enter heaven. An unrighteous and thus unholy human cannot dwell in the presence of a Holy God, according to His established order. This is why God sent His Son the Messiah to die for us. It is through His sacrificial atonement and our faith in that atonement that we are now made righteous and clean to enter heaven.

Consider these passages from the book of Romans:

- Romans 3:10: "There is no one righteous—no, not one."

- Romans 3:23-25: "For all have sinned and fall short of the glory of God. They are set right as a gift of His grace, through the redemption that is in Messiah Yeshua. God set forth Yeshua as an atonement, through faith in His blood, to show His righteousness in passing over sins already committed."

- Romans 5:8: "God demonstrates His own love toward us, in that while we were yet sinners, Messiah [Christ] died for us."

- Romans 6:23: "For sin's payment is death, but God's gracious gift is eternal life in Messiah Yeshua [Jesus] our Lord."

- Romans 10:9-10: "If you confess with your mouth that Yeshua is Lord, and believe in your heart that God raised Him from the dead, you will be saved. For with the heart it is believed for righteousness, and with the mouth it is confessed for salvation."

In his book *The Heaven Answer Book,* Billy Graham writes, "By His death, Jesus paid the penalty for our sins. This alone gives us everlasting life with Him in Heaven." He goes on to explain:

Every sin we commit is an act of rebellion—a deliberate renunciation of God's rightful authority over us. But sin in serious for another reason: it ravages our souls, bringing heartache and brokenness into our lives. Most of all, it cuts us off from fellowship with God.

Because of God's great love for us, however, He provided the way for us to be forgiven and cleansed of our sins—and, ultimately, to spend eternity with Him. We could never cleanse ourselves; sin's stain is too deep. But God made our forgiveness possible by sending Jesus Christ [Messiah] into the world as the final and complete sacrifice for our sins. On the cross, Jesus took the divine judgment that you and I deserve. He died in our place. The Bible says, "For [Messiah] Christ died for sins once for all, the righteous for the unrighteous, to bring you to God" (1 Peter 3:18).[12]

In the Gospel of John, Yeshua Himself declares, "I am the way, the truth, and the life! No one comes to the Father except through Me" (John 14:6). What Yeshua means here is quite obvious. The Father dwells in heaven and the sole means of reaching heaven is through the mediation of the Son. In these few words, Yeshua explains His purpose for coming to earth and dying for us. This statement establishes the single most fundamental truth of New Testament faith—the way to eternal life is found through Jesus the Messiah and Him alone.

Acts 4:12 restates this same fundamental New Covenant doctrine: "There is salvation in *no one else,* for there is *no other name* under heaven given to mankind by which we must be saved!" Known as the Gospel Imperative, this declaration also establishes without question that God has provided only one way for salvation and entrance into heaven, and that way is solely through the person of Yeshua.

A New Testament verse that excites me about heaven is this gem from the apostle Paul: "Things no eye has seen and no ear has heard, that have not entered the heart of mankind—these things God has prepared for those who love Him" (1 Corinthians 2:9). The magnificence of heaven is beyond anything we can comprehend with our finite mind.

Another encouraging Scripture passage is found in the eighth chapter of Romans, "I consider that our present sufferings are not worth comparing with the glory that will be revealed in us. For the creation waits in eager expectation for the children of God to be revealed" (Romans 8:18-19 NIV).

In other words, you may be going through seemingly unbearable circumstances in your life. You may feel hopeless. You may even feel like you are living through hell on earth. But the Bible says all of this suffering pales when we consider the joys and splendor that await us in heaven. It all comes into perspective.

MORE ABOUT HEAVEN FROM THE NEW TESTAMENT

The eleventh chapter of the book of Hebrews is called "the faith chapter," because it discusses the faith that motivated great Bible heroes like Noah, Moses, Abraham, and others. The chapter also talks about the "heavenly city" these heroes longed to see—"the city that has foundations, whose architect and builder is God" (Hebrews 11:10).

The writer of Hebrews goes on:

> *All these people were still living by faith when they died. They did not receive the things promised; they only saw them and welcomed them from a distance, admitting that they were foreigners and strangers on earth. People who say such things show that they are looking for a country of their own. If they had been thinking of the country they had left, they would have had opportunity to return. Instead, they were longing for a better country—a heavenly one. Therefore God is not ashamed to be called their God, for he has prepared a city for them* (Hebrews 11:13-16 NIV).

The New Testament depicts heaven as a place filled with feasting and joy, as the Messiah is united with "His bride," those who have put their faith in Him throughout the ages. In chapter 19 of Revelation, the apostle John writes:

> *Then a voice came from the throne, saying: "Praise our God, all you His servants and all who fear Him, both the small and the great!" Then I heard something like the voice of a great multitude—like the roaring of rushing waters or like the rumbling of powerful thunder— saying, "Hallelujah! For Adonai Elohei-Tzva'ot reigns! Let us rejoice and be glad and give the glory to Him! For the wedding of the Lamb has come, and His bride has made herself ready. She was given fine linen to wear, bright and clean! For the fine linen is the righteous deeds of the kedoshim." Then the angel tells me, "Write: How fortunate are those who have been invited to the wedding banquet of the Lamb!"* (Revelation 19:5-9)

Three chapters later, the apostle gives us another awe-inspiring view of heaven:

> *Then the angel showed me a river of the water of life— bright as crystal, flowing from the throne of God and of the Lamb down the middle of the city's street. On either side of the river was a tree of life, bearing twelve kinds of fruit, yielding its fruit each month; and the leaves of the tree were for the healing of the nations. No longer will there be any curse. The throne of God and of the Lamb shall be in the city, and His servants shall serve Him. They shall see His face, and His name shall be*

on their foreheads. Night shall be no more, and people will have no need for lamplight or sunlight—for Adonai Elohim will shine on them. And they shall reign forever and ever! (Revelation 22:1-5)

In his book *The World to Come,* Messianic Rabbi Derek Leman writes, "God has given us more information about the World to Come than we might think." He believes that we can see the signs of this paradise all around us, and that "the desires of the heart point the way":

> A family enjoys a day hike in the clear mountain air. It is a sign. A woman enjoys a story of love found at last. It is a sign. A child looks lovingly at a picture in a storybook. It is a sign.
>
> We can experience signs every day, though we easily overlook them. We can be reminded a thousand times what the World to Come may be like. It is there in beauty. We can simply look at the face of our spouse and see a hint of heaven. We can curl our toes in green grass and know paradise is real. We hear a child's innocent laughter and we can imagine. We forget ourselves and fall into the joy of friends and conversation. We can imagine true companionship that will never end or lead to disappointment.[13]

TOO HEAVENLY MINDED?

The old cliché is that some people are too heavenly minded to be any earthly good. Karl Marx called religion "the opiate of the people" because he felt that a belief in heaven led to a passive acceptance of oppression here on earth. In other words, "I may be suffering now, but that's okay because I'll get pie in the sky later on."

But the truth is precisely the opposite. True Christians who believe in heaven have led the fight against all sorts of evil systems, including communism, Nazism, and racism here in the United States. Look, for example, at the role the black (and white) church played in this country's civil rights movement.

As C.S. Lewis wrote, "If you read history you will find that the Christians who did most for the present world were precisely those who thought most of the next. It is since Christians have largely ceased to think of the other world that they have become so ineffective in this."[14]

WHAT WILL WE BE LIKE IN HEAVEN?

Have you ever wondered, "What will I be like in heaven?" Will you be a disembodied soul? Pure energy? Or will you have a body similar to the one you have now?

The New Testament tells us that Yeshua's body was resurrected and walked out of the open tomb three days after He died at Passover. When He appeared to His disciples after His resurrection, the Bible says:

> They were startled and frightened, thinking they saw a ghost. He said to them, "Why are you troubled, and why do doubts rise in your minds? Look at my hands and my feet. It is I myself! Touch me and see; a ghost does not have flesh and bones, as you see I have." When he had said this, he showed them his hands and feet. And while they still did not believe it because of joy and

amazement, he asked them, "Do you have anything here to eat?" They gave him a piece of broiled fish, and he took it and ate it in their presence (Luke 24:37-43 NIV).

Apparently Yeshua had the same physical body He'd had as long as His friends had known Him. They knew immediately who He was. At the same time, it was different. It seems that He was able to walk through locked doors or walls, because John 20:26 (NIV) says, "A week later his disciples were in the house again, and Thomas was with them. Though the doors were locked, Jesus came and stood among them and said, 'Peace be with you!'"

When we get to heaven, will we have the same type of body Jesus had during the 40 days He spent on earth following His resurrection? John MacArthur thinks so.

Our glorified bodies will be united with glorified bodies at the final resurrection.... What will the perfected soul be like? The most obvious truth is that it will finally be perfectly free from evil forever. We will never again have a selfish desire or utter useless words. We will never perform another unkind deed or think any sinful thought. We will be perfectly liberated from our captivity to sin, and finally able to do that which is absolutely righteous, holy and perfect before God. Can you imagine yourself behaving in such an incredible way? I frankly have a hard time envisioning myself as utterly perfect. But there will be no imperfection in Heaven!

...the best picture of what we'll be like in Heaven is the resurrection body of Jesus. We will have a body fit for the full life of God to indwell and express itself forever. It can eat but won't need to. It will be a body that can move at will through space and matter. It will be ageless and not know pain, tears, sorrow, sickness, or death.

It will also be a body of brilliant splendor. Christ's [Messiah's] glorified body is described as shining like the sun in its strength (Revelation 1:16). And in an Old Testament promise, Scripture compares our glorified body to the shining of the moon and stars: "They that be wise shall shine as the brightness of the firmament; and they that turn many to righteousness as the stars forever and ever" (Daniel 12:3).[15]

C.S. Lewis adds to our understanding:

Confusion between Spirit and soul (or "ghost") has done much harm. Ghosts must be pictured, if we are to picture them at all, as shadowy and tenuous, for ghosts are half-men; one element abstracted from a creature that ought to have flesh. But Spirit, if pictured at all, must be pictured in the very opposite way. Neither God nor even the gods are "shadowy" in traditional imagination; even the human dead, when glorified in Christ, cease to be "ghosts" and become "saints." The difference of atmosphere which even now surrounds the words "I saw a ghost," and "I saw a saint"—all the pallor and insubstantiality of the one, all the gold and blue of the other—contains more wisdom than the whole libraries of "religion." If we must have a mental picture to symbolize Spirit, we should represent it as something heavier than matter.[16]

Lewis believed we are uncomfortable talking about things of the Spirit because we don't understand them the way we understand the physical world. He wrote that because of this, we expect biblical accounts of the resurrection to "tell of a risen life which is purely 'spiritual' in the negative sense of the word: that is we use the word 'spiritual' to mean not what is, but what is not. We mean a life without space, without history, without environment, with no sensuous elements in it. We also, in our heart of hearts, tend to slur over the risen *manhood* of Jesus, to conceive Him, after death, simply returning into Deity, so that the resurrection would be no more than the reversal of doing the Incarnation."[17]

Lewis was convinced that we will still be ourselves in the life beyond this one. We will be joyful, energetic, inquisitive, and passionate creatures—more fully alive than we have ever been on this side of eternity.

Randy Alcorn, founder and director of Eternal Perspective Ministries, wrote a best-selling book called, simply, *Heaven*.[18] In his book he took it upon himself to answer dozens of questions about heaven from a Christian point of view. Among them the following, slightly embellished:

Will we maintain our own destinies?

You will be you in heaven. Who else would you be? If Bob, a man on Earth, is no longer Bob when he gets to heaven, then, in fact, Bob did not go to heaven. If when I arrive in heaven I'm not the same person with the same identity, history, and memory, then I didn't go to heaven.

Will we recognize each other?

Scripture gives no indication of a memory wipe causing us not to recognize family and friends. [Apostle] Paul anticipated being with the Thessalonians in heaven, and it never occurred to him he wouldn't know them. In fact, if we wouldn't know our loved ones, the "comfort" of an afterlife reunion, taught in 1 Thessalonians 4:14-18, would be no comfort at all.

Will our pets be restored?

In her excellent book about heaven, Joni Eareckson Tada says, "If God brings our pets back to life, it wouldn't surprise me. It would be just like Him. It would be totally in keeping with His generous character.... Exorbitant. Excessive. Extravagant in grace after grace. Of all the dazzling discoveries and ecstatic pleasures heaven will hold for us, the potential of seeing Scrappy would be pure whimsy—utterly, joyfully, surprisingly superfluous.... Heaven is going to be a place that will refract and reflect in as many ways as possible the goodness of our great God, who delights in lavishing love on His children."

Will we know everything?

God alone is omniscient. When we die, we'll see things far more clearly, and we'll know much more than we do now, but we'll never know everything. In 1 Corinthians

13:12, we are told "For now we see in a mirror dimly, but then face to face. Now I know in part, but then I will know fully, even as I have been fully known."

Will we rest?

Our lives in heaven will include rest (Hebrews 4:1-11). *"'Blessed are the dead who die in the Lord from now on.' 'Yes,' says the Spirit, 'they will rest from their labor, for their deeds will follow them'"* (Revelation 14:13 NIV).

Will we work?

The idea of working in heaven is foreign to many people. Yet Scripture does indicate that work is part of God's divine plan for man. When God created Adam, He "took the man and put him in the Garden of Eden to work it and take care of it" (Genesis 2:15 NIV). Work was part of the original Eden. It was part of a perfect human life on Earth. But don't get too worried...we will thoroughly enjoy the work we are doing!

Will there be art, drama, and entertainment?

God is an inventor and the director of the unfolding drama of redemption. He created the universe, then wrote, directed, and took the leading role in history's greatest story. We who have lived our own dramas and participated in God's, we whose lives were enriched through drama, should recognize its value in the new universe. The quality of drama will likely be vastly improved.

Will we laugh?

"If you're not allowed to laugh in Heaven, I don't want to go there." It wasn't Mark Twain who said that. It was Martin Luther.

Where did humor originate? Not with people, angels, or Satan. God created all good things, including good humor. If God didn't have a sense of humor, we as His image-bearers wouldn't. That He has a sense of humor is evident in His creation. Consider aardvarks and baboons. Take a good look at a giraffe. You have to smile, don't you?

I've only taken a few sentences from Alcorn's in-depth answers to questions about heaven. And I've included only a smattering of the questions he tackles in his 516-page book, which is well worth further study.

FURTHER NEW TESTAMENT THOUGHTS ABOUT HEAVEN

Do not let your hearts be troubled. You believe in God; believe also in me. My Father's house has many rooms; if that were not so, would I have told you that I am going there to prepare a place for you? And if I go and prepare a place for you, I will come back and take you to be with me that you also may be where I am (John 14:1-3 NIV).

The New Testament uses the word "heaven" 275 times. Yeshua told many parables about heaven, spoke about the qualities that are necessary for entrance into heaven, and, in beautiful passages like the one in John 14, assured His followers that a life free from trouble and pain awaits at the end of this life.

Another of Yeshua's beautiful teachings on heaven is found in the Lord's Prayer, which most know from the King James Version of the Scriptures:

> *Our Father which art in heaven, hallowed be thy name.*
> *Thy kingdom come, thy will be done in earth, as it is in*
> *heaven* (Matthew 6:9-10).

In these two poetic sentences, the Messiah teaches us two important truths. The first is that there is a place, a real place, called heaven and that God Almighty dwells there. The second is that God's will is to be done in the here and now, just as it is done in heaven. This is a powerful echo of the Jewish concept of a homeland over which God the Creator rules.

Yeshua had much more to say about heaven, some of it admittedly hard to understand. From Matthew 22 comes this parable:

> *The kingdom of heaven is like a king who prepared a*
> *wedding banquet for his son. He sent his servants to*
> *those who had been invited to the banquet to tell them*
> *to come, but they refused to come.*
>
> *Then he sent some more servants and said, "Tell those*
> *who have been invited that I have prepared my dinner:*
> *My oxen and fattened cattle have been butchered, and*
> *everything is ready. Come to the wedding banquet."*
>
> *But they paid no attention and went off—one to his*
> *field, another to his business. The rest seized his servants,*

mistreated them and killed them. The king was enraged. He sent his army and destroyed those murderers and burned their city.

Then he said to his servants, "The wedding banquet is ready, but those I invited did not deserve to come. So go to the street corners and invite to the banquet anyone you find." So the servants went out into the streets and gathered all the people they could find, the bad as well as the good, and the wedding hall was filled with guests.

But when the king came in to see the guests, he noticed a man there who was not wearing wedding clothes. He asked, "How did you get in here without wedding clothes, friend?" The man was speechless.

Then the king told the attendants, "Tie him hand and foot, and throw him outside, into the darkness, where there will be weeping and gnashing of teeth.

"For many are invited, but few are chosen" (Matthew 22:2-13 NIV).

Yeshua seems to be telling us that we will find many people in heaven who we don't expect to be there. As the redeemed slave trader John Newton said, "If I ever reach heaven I expect to find three wonders there. First, to meet some I had not thought to see there. Second, to miss some I had expected to see there. And third, the greatest wonder of all, to find myself there."

But what about the man who is thrown out because he is not dressed in wedding clothes? He is the one who has never accepted the garment of salvation offered by faith in Yeshua's atoning death, burial, and resurrection. He thinks he should be there, he may have lived a good life, so he thinks. Perhaps his numerous good deeds outweighed his bad? Still, it wasn't enough and he was cast out.

Another of Yeshua's parables has a clear reference to the judgment that will come at the end of the age:

> The kingdom of heaven is like a man who sowed good seed in his field. But while everyone was sleeping, his enemy came and sowed weeds among the wheat, and went away. When the wheat sprouted and formed heads, then the weeds also appeared.
>
> The owner's servants came to him and said, "Sir, didn't you sow good seed in your field? Where then did the weeds come from?"
>
> "An enemy did this," he replied.
>
> The servants asked him, "Do you want us to go and pull them up?"
>
> "No," he answered, "because while you are pulling the weeds, you may uproot the wheat with them. Let both grow together until the harvest. At that time I will tell the harvesters: First collect the weeds and tie them in bundles to be burned; then gather the wheat and bring it into my barn" (Matthew 13:24-30 NIV).

Although taught in allegorical form, this parable seems to indicate that all of us will face a divine separation and judgment after death. The wheat here refers to the righteous who will be judged worthy and eventually enter the barn (heaven) and the weeds who are found to be unworthy and will be "bundled to be burned." I'll talk more about this group in the next section.

Yeshua also emphasized the importance of focusing on heaven over living a lavish life on earth: "Sell your possessions and give to the poor. Provide purses for yourselves that will not wear out, a treasure in heaven that will never fail, where no thief comes near and no moth destroys" (Luke 12:33 NIV).

And He said of Himself, "I am the living bread that came down from heaven. Whoever eats this bread will live forever. This bread is my flesh, which I will give for the life of the world" (John 6:51 NIV).

Yeshua continues to make the claim that He is the One sent to provide eternal life and entrance into heaven. John 3:16, perhaps the most famous verse in the New Testament, again echoes this truth: "For God so loved the world that he gave his one and only Son, that whoever believes in him shall not perish but have eternal life."

The apostle John underscored the fact that the ministry of Yeshua was about securing a place for His followers in heaven, there to enjoy fellowship with His Father, the God of Abraham, Isaac, and Jacob for eternity. Just in case John 3:16 isn't clear enough, he settles the issue beyond any doubt in verse 36 of the same chapter: "Whoever believes in the Son has eternal life, but whoever rejects the Son will not see life, for God's wrath remains on them."

Here are offered both an explicit promise and a warning— heaven or hell. The choice was up to those with ears to hear. It is a powerful statement echoed time and again in the New Testament.

Other New Testament references to heaven range from advice and admonition on how to get there to vivid descriptions of the place itself. For example, in Matthew 18:10 Yeshua gathers the little children to Himself in order to illustrate what is required for citizenship in heaven: "See that you do not despise one of these little ones," He told His followers. "For I tell you that their angels in heaven always see the face of my Father who is in heaven."

In Philippians 3:20-21, Paul declares that those who believe in Yeshua are already citizens of heaven through their faith: "Our citizenship is in heaven, and from there we eagerly wait for the Savior, the Lord Yeshua the Messiah. He will transform this humble body of ours into the likeness of His glorious body, through the power that enables Him even to put all things in subjection to Himself."

This is clearly a statement of staggering importance. Paul says, in effect, that Yeshua will literally transform our physical bodies at the time of resurrection and, further, that we will be in eternal fellowship with Him in heaven. With these few words, Paul affirms both the doctrines of resurrection and of the existence God's kingdom in the afterlife.

As we conclude our discussion of what the New Testament says about heaven, I want to turn back to the book of Revelation, where the apostle John provides an awe-inspiring account of heaven's reality. I quoted extensively from Revelation in the previous chapter, but want to build on that here.

Written while John was banished to exile on the Isle of Patmos for faith in the Messiah, Revelation is part of a long tradition of Jewish apocalyptic literature. At the time John wrote his extraordinary account, many other Jewish prophets were also committing their dreams and visions to parchment and sheepskins. Few of these prophetic works have come down to us today, but John's description of the vision God gave him on Patmos endures, thanks largely to its unforgettable depiction of the majesty and wonder of heaven, as John was privileged to see it with human eyes.

Then the angel showed me the river of the water of life, as clear as crystal, flowing from the throne of God and of the Lamb down the middle of the great street of the city. On each side of the river stood the tree of life, bearing twelve crops of fruit, yielding its fruit every month. And the leave of the tree are for the healing of the nations. No longer will there be any curse. The throne of God and of the Lamb will be in the city, and his servants will serve him. They will see his face, and his name will be on their foreheads. There will be no more night. They will not need the light of a lamp or the light of the sun, for the Lord God will give them light. And they will reign for ever and ever (Revelation 22:1-5 NIV).

There couldn't possibly be a more inspiring, exciting, or edifying description of our destiny in the afterlife. The only other verses that compare in stirring our imagination and instructing us as to our eternal choice in this life are those that deal directly with the reality of hell. It is to that dark and infernal place that we turn our attention in the next section.

Part Three

HELL

Chapter 6

IS HELL FOR REAL?

LYING HELPLESS IN A Paris hospital, suffering from a grave abdominal condition, 42-year-old Howard Storm had only one thought: *How long will it take me to die?*

An atheist, Howard believed that when death came, he would simply cease to exist. And so, confident of his final fate and weary of the fight, Howard said goodbye to his wife, closed his eyes, and waited for oblivion.

A few moments later, Howard awoke. Much to his shock, not only was he very much alive, but he was no longer lying *in* his hospital bed. Instead he was standing *by* it. On top of that, his senses were super charged. He could hear his own blood rushing through his veins, smell the chlorine on the sheets, and feel every slight movement of air against his skin. In the midst of this sensory overload, a bright light suddenly flooded the room.

He tried repeatedly to communicate to his wife, but she never responded. Instead, she remained glued to her chair, her head bowed, softly crying—seemingly oblivious to his existence. His efforts to communicate with his wife proving futile, Howard looked down at the bed next to him. There, lying in *his* hospital bed, was a large motionless lump. Howard took a step closer, and as he did, a wave of horror swept over him: *Dear God, that lump is me!*

In shock, Howard braced himself against the hospital room wall. That's when he heard the hushed voices. At first he was unsure from where they were coming. But as he walked toward the door, he realized they were coming from down the hallway...even more bizarre, they were calling his name!

"Howard, Howard...come out here," they beckoned in perfect English—with absolutely no trace of a French accent. Way down at the end of the strangely grey and misty hall, he vaguely made out the outline of four or five people...their hands extended and fingers motioning him to follow them. "Howard, come on. We've been waiting for you for such a *long* time. We can help you," they pleaded.

Unsure at first what to do, Howard stood in the doorway—anxious about leaving the security of his hospital room. Finally, he started toward the voices. Fighting a gnawing sense of fear, Howard told himself to "get a grip." Who else could they be but hospital staff?

Despite his attempts to reassure himself, with each step he took, the sense of foreboding increased. The voices, sensing his hesitancy, became impatient—even, he was noticing with not a little concern, a bit surly.

"Howard, you *have* to come with us...*now!*"

Howard kept walking, fearful but strangely fascinated. Inexplicably, the longer he walked, the darker the hallway seemed to get.

Then in a flash—he didn't know how or why—the thought came to him that it was all a ruse. Those people were not there to help him. They were there to hurt him. Before he could even process that thought, Howard suddenly stumbled as the hallway took a slight dip and darkness enveloped him.

Instantly, Howard was bombarded with a barrage of the foulest language he had ever heard. Realizing his horrible mistake, Howard quickly turned to go back to his hospital room. Immediately, he was savagely attacked.

Trying to defend himself, he swung back like a wild man. It was futile. There in the pitch-black darkness, he could feel their solid bodies pressing against him. Only now, instead of a few, there were hordes of them, jeering as they surrounded him like a pack of wild dogs. With their long nails and sharp teeth, they began to bite and tear at his flesh. To his horror he realized that he was being taken apart and eaten alive! And that's when he knew. The nihilists, the atheists, the skeptics...they had all been wrong. Dead wrong. There was no oblivion, no annihilation, and no end of existence when a person left this world.

I'll tell you more of Howard Storm's story when we get to the final section of this book. Storm, a former atheist and college professor, is one of several Near-Death Experience survivors I interviewed on my television show, *Jewish Voice with Jonathan Bernis*. Storm, who is now an ordained minister, says he went to hell, or at least hell's waiting room, and I believe him.

Even today, Howard visibly recoils when he starts to share his encounter with the demonic—unable to tell most of what happened to him because it was, in his words, "invasive and disgusting." He is also one of those who completely changed his lifestyle, transforming from strident atheist to church pastor. In fact, the change was so dramatic that his first wife left him. She hadn't signed up to be a preacher's wife and, apparently, missed the fun they had when they were swingers who didn't fear God—or hell.

Now, let me admit that I would prefer to believe that there's no such place as hell. I hate to think of anyone spending an eternity in torment. (Anyone, that is, except perhaps Adolf Hitler or other brutal dictators or mass murderers.) But the truth is that it doesn't matter one iota what I believe. Hell won't disappear just because I don't believe in it. Today, a lot of people are writing books saying that hell doesn't exist. But that doesn't change anything.

In his book *The Case for Faith,* Lee Strobel interviewed Dr. J.P. Moreland, a professor of philosophy and ethics who wrote the book *Beyond Death: Exploring the Evidence for Immortality.* When Strobel asks whether the creation of hell calls God's character into question, Moreland replies:

> Actually, hell was not part of the original creation. Hell is God's fall-back position. Hell is something God was forced to make because people chose to rebel against him and turn against what was best for them and the purpose for which they were created.
>
> You know, when people founded the United States, they didn't start out by creating jails. They would have much rather had a society without jails. But they were forced to create them because people would not cooperate. The same is true for hell.[1]

Strobel also quotes theologian D.A. Carson:

> Hell is not a place where people are consigned because they're pretty good blokes, but they just didn't believe the right stuff. They're consigned there, first and foremost, because they deny their maker and want to be at the center of the universe. Hell is not filled with people who have already repented, only God isn't gentle enough, or good enough, to let them out. It's filled with people who, for all eternity, still want to be the center of the universe and who persist in their God-defying rebellion.
>
> What is God to do? If he says it doesn't matter to him then God is no longer a God to be admired. He's either amoral or positively creepy. For him to act in any other way in the face of such blatant defiance would be to reduce God himself.[2]

C.S. Lewis goes so far as to suggest that those who wind up in hell are there by their own choice: "I willingly believe that the damned are, in one sense, successful rebels to the end; that the doors of Hell are locked on the inside...."[3]

In his book *The Great Divorce,* C.S. Lewis writes about men who are unable to accept the truth even when it is right in front of them. They are always learning, debating, but never coming to a conclusion about anything, even when their eternal destination seems to hang in the balance. In the following conversation, one of "the Bright People"—a spirit from Heaven—is talking to a "fat ghost" who has found himself in Hell, but doesn't seem to be aware of it:

"You can begin as if nothing had ever gone wrong. White as snow. It's all true, you know. He is in me, for you, with that power. And—I have come a long journey to meet you. You have seen Hell; you are in sight of Heaven. Will you, even now, repent and believe?"

"I'm not sure that I've got the exact point you are trying to make," said the Ghost.

"I am not trying to make any point," said the Spirit. "I am telling you to repent and believe."

"But my dear boy, I believe already. We may not be perfectly agreed, but you have completely misjudged me if you do not realise that my religion is a very real and a very precious thing to me."

"Very well," said the other, as if changing his plan. "Will you believe in me?"

"In what sense?"

"Will you come with me to the mountains? It will hurt at first, until your feet are hardened. Reality is harsh to the feet of shadows. But will you come?"

When the Ghost is told that he will see the face of God if he comes, he replies:

"Ah, but we must all interpret those beautiful words in our own way! For me there is no such thing as a final answer. The free wind of inquiry must always continue to blow through the mind, must it not? 'Prove all things'…to travel hopefully is better than to arrive.

"If that were true, and known to be true, how could anyone travel hopefully? There would be nothing to hope for."

"But you must feel yourself that there is something stifling about the idea of finality. Stagnation, my dear boy, what is more soul-destroying than stagnation?"[4]

Look through history and you'll see that humankind has just about always believed in a hell of some kind.

Ancient man apprehended ancient truths about heaven and hell as if "through a glass darkly" (1 Corinthians 13:12 KJV). Over the ages, that glass has become clearer and less opaque. Myths and legends mix and meld, fragments and pieces joined together, the whole is revealed through the parts.

Even in the teeming polytheistic world of the Egyptian Empire, we see dim traces of the reality of hell. During the height of the Egyptian Middle Kingdom, and the rise of the cult of Osiris, moral righteousness became the dominant factor in determining a person's suitability for eternal life. It was said that at death a person faced judgment by a tribunal of forty-two divine judges. If the dead person had led a life in conformance with the precepts of the goddess Maat, who represented truth and right living, he or she was welcomed into paradise. If found guilty of an immoral lifestyle, the person was thrown to a "devourer," to be tortured and then annihilated.

It's interesting to note that in ancient Egypt the doctrine of eternal punishment did not exist. The underworld, to the Egyptians, was simply the abode of the dead, a vast repository of lost souls who would eventually cease to exist altogether.

This notion of an indeterminate way-station—where the dead wandered aimlessly through a desolate landscape, forever separated from the land of the living—stretches deep into prehistory. The ancient Middle Eastern cultures of Mesopotamia, including Samaria, Babylonia, and Assyria, reveal some of the earliest evidence for the concept of the netherworld. It is this little understood realm that appears in such ancient texts as the *Epic of Gilgamesh*, *Descent of Inanna to the Netherworld*, *Baal and the Underworld*, and *The Descent of Ishtar.*

Greeks emulated both the Egyptians and the great Middle Eastern cultures in their concept of the underworld. In classic Greek mythology, a place called Tartarus was conceived as a deep, dismal world beneath the earth, an abyss used as a dungeon to torment those who had been consigned there. Tartarus was considered to be only a small part of the larger realm of the underworld, known as Hades. In his treatise, *Gorgias,* written in the fourth century B.C., Plato posited that souls sent to Tartarus had been judged for their earthly deeds.

So it was across the rest of the ancient world as humankind struggled to understand what awaited departed souls in the world beyond this one. Examples abound. In pagan Europe, what might be called proto-hells included Anaon from Breton mythology, the Celtic Uffern, and the Slavic Peklo. In ancient Indian mythology, the place of punishment for condemned souls was called Kalachi or Naraka, while the folklore of the Asian Ainu tribe described hell as a subterranean place with perpetually dripping water.

Among the more interesting variations on early concepts of the afterlife is that of the African Serer religion, which combined both elements of ancestor worship with an early idea of a posthumous place of punishment. For the Serer people, heaven is described as being accepted after death by one's beloved ancestors. To be rejected by the ancestors for evil deeds committed in life turns one into a wandering soul who must make his way to a sacred dwelling place to redeem his destiny. Those unable or unwilling to make the journey live all eternity as lost souls.

Hell also appeared often in the mythology of the ancient religions of North, Central, and South America. The Mayans conceived of Xibalba, a fierce and loathsome place with nine levels ruled by fierce demons.

The Aztecs, on the other hand, subscribed to belief in a place called Mictlan. After death, the souls of the departed journeyed for four years to reach this land, overcoming difficult and demanding tests along the way. These included crossing a range of mountains that crashed into each other, a field across which blew a wind of flesh-piercing knives, and a river of blood swarming with ferocious jaguars.

These are just a few of the examples of primitive concepts of hell that have been passed down to us through the ages. Most, if not all it seems, struggled with the virtually universal notion that there was a place consigned to the evildoer where he would pay for his sins after death. Simply put, the reality of hell has been vividly present in nearly every culture and civilization that has flourished and withered on the face of the earth. Hell seems to be a reality that humanity has been groping to understand from time immemorial.

With the emergence of the world's major religions, that struggle for understanding continued. Islamic belief follows that of Judeo-Christian doctrine in many particulars. Hell in the Koran is called Jahannam, which is closely related to the Hebrew word *gehinnom*. Both heaven and hell, according to the Koran, are divided into a myriad of levels, to which saints and sinners are respectively con-signed. Although Islamic belief generally portrays hell as a burning, steaming cave of horrors, there is another tradition that describes it as a place of unbearable cold, wracked with blizzards, ice, and snow. The lowest pits of the Islamic hell are reserved for the hypocrites who proclaim the name of Allah and his messenger but reject both in their hearts. Its gates are guarded by an angel named Maalik.

Predictably, both Buddhist and Hindu doctrine present an intricate, densely hierarchical depiction of hell, closely tied to the cycles of reincarnation and rebirth. Buddhist theology teaches that there are five levels of rebirth, the lowest of which is a realm of "endless suffering." However, as with all stages of rebirth, hell and its suffering are not permanent.

Vedic religion, upon which Hinduism is founded, speaks of a realm similar to classic concepts of hell. Called naraka, it is pre-sided over by the god Yamaraja, who holds court to judge the sins of newly arrived souls. A record keeper, Chutragupta, reads out the offenses and appropriate punishments are handed down. Pun-ishments include being dipped in boiling oil, burned in fire, and tortured with various infernal instruments. Once the punishment is applied, the suffering soul is allowed to be reborn. Yet again, the concept of endless punishment is not an element in these depictions of the afterlife.

One element that is shared, however, in many of these ancient portrayals of hell is the horrific and ghastly torture awaiting those who are consigned to this terrible place. In Chinese folk myths, for example, suffering souls are sawn in half, beheaded, hurled into pits of filth, and forced to climb trees bristling with razor-sharp blades. Once a soul has atoned for its sins by suffering such tortures, it is given the "Drink of Forgetfulness" and allowed to be reborn, sent back into the world as an animal or sick, poor individual, taking another turn on the cosmic wheel of reincarnation.

The sacred writings of Zoroastrianism make mention of a place beyond death called The House of the Lie. It is here that "those that are of evil dominion, of evil deeds, of evil words, of evil self and evil thoughts" are likewise sent to atone for their misdeeds. Often, in Zoroastrian theology, the punishment closely fits the crime. For example, those who treated work animals cruelly in life will be trampled by cattle as punishment. As vivid as these depictions are, they come short of describing punishment an eternity. In fact, Zoroastrian eschatology describes a 1,000-year era, after which three saviors will journey to hell, resurrecting the suffering souls there to perfection.

And so it goes. The complex, contradictory roads that lead to our modern concept of hell pass through virtually every stage of civilization, revealing along the way a rich tapestry of mythic and imaginative speculation as to the nature and final disposition of those souls who have, in life, fallen short of the moral and ethical expectations of their societies. It is significant to point out that many of these depictions contain elements of the truth—a truth that was finally and fully revealed in Judeo-Christian theological and philosophical speculation.

Nonetheless, according to a recent Pew Forum on Religion and Public Life survey, only 59 percent of Americans believe in hell. That's fewer than six out of ten people. And though that would seem to make that a narrow majority of people who believe in hell, another poll narrowed that question down and discovered that fewer than half of all Americans (43 percent) think that people go to hell based on their actions on earth.

N.T. Wright is Anglican Bishop of Durham, England. He has taught New Testament Studies at Oxford, Cambridge, and McGill University, and writes:

> I was congratulated not long ago, on the basis of selective quotations from my writings, on being a universalist, that is, on believing that all humans will be saved, including Adolf Hitler and Osama bin Laden. That, however, is not the position I take, or have ever taken. The New Testament is full of sober and serious warnings of the real possibility of final loss, and I do not think they are merely rhetorical devices to frighten us ahead of time into a salvation which will in fact come to all sooner or later....[5]

Writing about New Testament Scriptures that focus on hell and eternal punishment, Bishop Wright says, "It is hard to see how we can ignore such passages...without being accused of trimming our theology to suit the prevailing desire to be nice to everybody, never to say anything that implies that someone might be in danger."[6]

Pastor Brian Jones, author of *Hell is Real (but I Hate to Admit It)*, says, "In 25 years of being a pastor, I would say that *maybe* 3 out of 10 Christians I've met *truly* believe people who die without becoming Christians go to hell."[7]

Jones himself was once one of those people. Although he has always been an evangelical Christian, at one point during his ministry, he "secretly" gave up on hell altogether. There were many reasons for this decision, not the least of which was that he was simply too embarrassed to preach on a doctrine that would make him, "lose friends and influence no one."

"One of the biggest things that weighed on me was how cruel and arrogant the concept of hell sounded when I talked about it with good friends of mine who weren't Christians," states Jones. "Though I'm loathe to admit this now, I tended to agree with Victor Hugo (author of *Les Misérables*) when he wrote, 'Hell is an outrage on humanity. When you tell me that your deity made you in his image, I reply that he must have been very ugly.'"[8]

Jones' position on hell was changed, however, after a powerful supernatural encounter while on a personal, yearly retreat in a monastery. Feeling a strange sense of spiritual pressure—a feeling that he described as "being underwater"—Jones began to pray… only to find his prayers "bouncing off the ceiling." God wasn't answering and Jones—who by this time had sequestered himself in a cold, cement-block room—wanted to know why. Because God's nature is such that He loves to give us the desire of our hearts—especially if those desires happen to coincide with His own—six hours later, God answered. What He told Jones shocked him: *"Brian, this charade has to end. You're a pastor and your job is to teach the Bible, but you don't believe what you're teaching. You don't believe in hell."*[9]

For the next five hours, Jones read and underlined every passage about hell that he could find in the Scriptures. By the time he was through with his "investigative report," an overwhelming sense of conviction came over him—causing him to throw himself on the cold, hard cement—face down—on the monastery floor.

That horrible place called hell—that reprehensible, disgusting, worm-infested, teeth-gnashing fiery pit of everlasting darkness—wasn't just mentioned here and there in a few scattered Bible verses; rather it was taught *everywhere*, Jones discovered.

In the book of Matthew alone, Jones discovered, hell is taught in twelve separate passages and summarized in Matthew 13:49-50 (NIV): "This is how it will be at the end of the age. The angels will come and separate the wicked from the righteous and throw them into the blazing furnace, where there will be weeping and gnashing of teeth."

"Blazing furnace?" "Weeping?" "Gnashing of teeth?" Those uncomfortable descriptions of a place of torment made Jones "fully persuaded" that a place of eternal conscious torment did, in fact, exist. Even worse…millions would be going there.

After spending several hours on the cold monastery floor—weeping bitter tears of repentance before God—Jones knew he had to warn people. He called his congregation together for a special meeting. Their reaction—or more accurately—"non-reaction"? Blank stares…followed by, "You really scared me. I thought you called us all together to tell us that you did something serious, like have an affair."[10]

Apparently, it's difficult for some people to get worked up about hell. But what would you do if you woke up one morning, looked out your window, and saw that your neighbor's house was on fire?

Would you roll over and go back to sleep, telling yourself that it's none of your business? Of course not! First of all, you'd call 911 and tell the operator that firefighters were needed immediately. Then you'd rush over to your neighbor's house and start banging on the door to make sure they got out while they could.

A person would have to be awfully callous and selfish to turn away when his neighbors were in such desperate peril.

This example illustrates the seriousness, even the urgency of this often-avoided subject. If we believe in the truth of the Scriptures, then we are compelled to deal with the reality of a place called hell. Yes, it is a terrible notion, one I would personally choose to avoid... if I could. But as one who has come to believe in the authority of the Bible, both Old and New Testaments, I cannot hide from the numerous warnings I read on its pages. And I challenge you not to hide from this topic either.

Your eternal destiny may depend on it.

Chapter 7

ANCIENT AND MODERN
JEWISH VIEWS OF HELL

WE JEWISH PEOPLE LOVE to tell stories. So I'll begin our investigation of the Jewish view of hell with a tale that has been passed down through the centuries. Rabbi Haim of Romshishok was an itinerant preacher. He traveled from town to town delivering religious sermons that stressed the importance of respect for one's fellow man. He often began his talks with the following story:

> I once ascended to the firmaments. I first went to see hell and the sight was horrifying. Row after row of tables were laden with platters of sumptuous food, yet the people seated around the tables were pale and emaciated, moaning in hunger. As I came closer, I understood their predicament.

Every person held a full spoon, but both arms were splinted with wooden slats so he could not bend either elbow to bring the food to his mouth. It broke my heart to hear the tortured groans of these poor people as they held their food so near but could not consume it.

Next I went to visit heaven. I was surprised to see the same setting I had witnessed in hell—row after row of long tables laden with food. But in contrast to hell, the people here in heaven were sitting contentedly talking with each other, obviously sated from their sumptuous meal. As I came closer, I was amazed to discover that here, too, each person had his arms splinted on wooden slats that prevented him from bending his elbows. How, then, did they manage to eat?

As I watched, a man picked up his spoon and dug it into the dish before him. Then he stretched across the table and fed the person across from him! The recipient of this kindness thanked him and returned the favor by leaning across the table to feed his benefactor.

I suddenly understood. Heaven and hell had the same circumstances and conditions. The critical difference is in the way the people treat each other.

I ran back to hell to share this solution with the poor souls trapped there. I whispered in the ear of one starving man, "You do not have to go hungry. Use your spoon to feed your neighbor, and he will surely return the favor and feed you."

"You expect me to feed the detestable man sitting across the table?" asked the man angrily. "I would rather starve than give him the pleasure of eating!"

I then understood God's wisdom in choosing who is worthy to go to heaven and who deserves to go to hell.

As with many Jewish folktales, legends, and parables, there is much to ponder here, wrapped up in an enjoyable and subtly ironic tale. For centuries, Jewish wisdom has been dispensed with wit and humor.

I don't think any of us would dispute that there is evil in this world. Real, tangible evil. We see it all around us. Bigotry, hatred, genocide. No other people have experienced this reality more than the Jewish people. For the Jews, evil is not an abstraction. It has a name. Many names, in fact—Auschwitz, Dachau, Buchenwald, and other death camps scattered across Eastern Europe. It was here that the Jews experienced pure evil, and emerged as survivors of one of the darkest chapters in human history. For those survivors and many who have experienced such horrific evil, it feels like hell is here on earth. But the Bible tells of a very real place of evil and suffering far beyond what anyone has ever experienced in this life.

HELL IN THE TANAKH

The Jewish Scriptures have many references to a place of punishment in the afterlife. Confusion arises from modern translations of these ancient passages.

For example, the word *Hades* appears often in early Jewish writing and is, in fact, a direct borrowing from the Greek. In Hellenistic mythology, Hades was the god of the underworld, whose name eventually became synonymous with the abode of the dead. Hades, in Jewish literature, is a place where the departed wander in dank and dim caves, dressed in rags and mourning their former lives. It seems likely that the early translators simply used Hades as a convenient term for other words that appeared in Jewish texts.

Whether or not the sages and scholars who wrote these texts actually intended to invoke the classical Greek definition of the word remains a matter of speculation. Nevertheless, the term Hades took on common usage as the ancient Jewish writings were translated and retranslated. Is Hades the same as hell? Not exactly. Jewish descriptions of Hades do not include mention of wicked souls, eternal or otherwise. It seems that it was, instead, simply a vast realm populated by the ghosts of the dead, with no reference to their deeds while on earth.

The second term that is also used frequently in the Tanakh is *Sheol*. The term is used 65 times in the Old Testament. In the 1611 King James Version of the Bible, 31 of those occurrences are translated as "hell," another 31 as "grave," and the remaining three as "pit." This misuse of the word has increased confusion about the real meaning of the word.

Sheol is not the same as the grave, which is *kever* in Hebrew. The ancient Jews believed that when a person died, his or her body went to the grave, but their soul went to Sheol. Neither is Sheol the same as hell. Like Hades, it was not necessarily thought to be a place of punishment. Rather, it was an abode for all the dead.

The word *Sheol* is found for the first time in chapter 37 of Genesis. I'm sure you remember the story. A young man named Joseph is hated by his older brothers because he is clearly their father's favorite son. Out in the fields one day, they see their chance to get rid of the pest. After selling him as a slave for twenty shekels of silver, they dip his coat in the blood of a newly killed goat. Then they tell their father, Jacob, that they found the coat this way, and that Joseph must have been attacked and killed by a lion or other wild animal.

When Jacob hears the tragic news, he weeps and says, "I will go down to Sheol in mourning for my son" (Genesis 37:35 New American Standard Bible).

Some versions of the Scriptures translate this passage as, "I will down to the grave." But this is not what Jacob said. After all, he thought Joseph had been killed by a wild animal and was not in a grave. Jacob expects to be reunited with his lost son when his soul enters into Sheol. Jacob believed that his son's body was dead—but he believed that his soul was still alive in Sheol and that they would be reunited after death.

It may be possible that those in Sheol were sometimes allowed to contact the living. A startling example of this may have occurred in chapter 28 of the Old Testament book of 1 Samuel. King Saul seeks out a medium known as the Witch of Endor and asks her to summon the spirit of the prophet Samuel. The Bible tells the story this way:

> *When Saul saw the Philistine army, he was afraid; terror filled his heart. He inquired of the Lord, but the Lord did not answer him by dreams or Urim or prophets.*

Saul then said to his attendants, "Find me a woman who is a medium, so I may go and inquire of her."

"There is one in Endor," they said.

So Saul disguised himself, putting on other clothes, and at night he and two men went to the woman. "Consult a spirit for me," he said, "and bring up for me the one I name."

But the woman said to him, "Surely you know what Saul has done. He has cut off the mediums and spiritists from the land. Why have you set a trap for my life to bring about my death?"

Saul swore to her by the Lord, "As surely as the Lord lives, you will not be punished for this."

Then the woman asked, "Whom shall I bring up for you?"

"Bring up Samuel," he said.

When the woman saw Samuel, she cried out at the top of her voice and said to Saul, "Why have you deceived me? You are Saul!"

The king said to her, "Don't be afraid. What do you see?"

The woman said, "I see a ghostly figure coming up out of the earth."

"What does he look like?" he asked.

"An old man wearing a robe is coming up," she said.

Then Saul knew it was Samuel, and he bowed down and prostrated himself with his face to the ground.

Samuel said to Saul, "Why have you disturbed me by bringing me up?"

"I am in great distress," Saul said. "The Philistines are fighting against me, and God has departed from me. He no longer answers me, either by prophets or by dreams. So I have called on you to tell me what to do."

Samuel said, "Why do you consult me, now that the Lord has departed from you and become your enemy? The Lord has done what he predicted through me. The Lord has torn the kingdom out of your hands and given it to one of your neighbors—to David" (1 Samuel 28:5-17 NIV).

A WORD OF WARNING

Bible commentators are divided on whether or not this was actually the departed spirit of Samuel or an imposter, an evil spirit claiming to be Samuel. Either way, it's important to point out that Saul was disobeying God when he sought advice from the dead. The Bible is clear on the subject:

Let no one be found among you who...practices divination or sorcery, interprets omens, engages in witchcraft, or casts spells, or who is a medium or spiritist or who consults the dead. Anyone who does these things is detestable to the Lord... (Deuteronomy 18:10-12 NIV).

Do not turn to mediums or seek out spiritists, for you will be defiled by them. I am the Lord your God (Leviticus 19:31 NIV).

A man or a woman who is a medium or a spiritist among you must be put to death. You are to stone them; their blood will be on their own hands (Leviticus 20:27 NIV).

When someone tells you to consult mediums and spiritists, who whisper and mutter, should not a people inquire of their God? Why consult the dead on behalf of the living? (Isaiah 8:19 NIV)

Why is God so strong in His condemnation of these practices? The Bible doesn't really say—but my opinion is that there are primarily two reasons for this. The first is that ancestor worship was so prevalent in the ancient world—and still is today in some regions. God alone belongs on the throne. He will not share it. He says, "You shall have no other gods before me" (Exodus 20:3), and that includes those who have passed from this world.

The second reason is that trying to contact the dead opens a person up to deception and influence from demons. In other words, those who attempt to contact the dead actually wind up in communication with demons who are merely impersonating the dead. There are many reasons why I believe this is so, but that's a subject for another time and place. For now, I felt that I must at least include a warning about the trouble people can get themselves into when they try to contact the dead for any reason. Demons are real...and they are dangerous.

Consider the story of Elisabeth Kübler-Ross, the author of the watershed book *On Death and Dying*. When she died in 2004, *The New York Times* said that her "pioneering work with terminally ill patients helped to revolutionize attitudes toward the care of the dying."

Dr. Kübler-Ross was probably best-known for outlining the stages people go through when they discover they have a terminal disease: 1) Denial, 2) Anger, 3) Bargaining, 4) Depression, 5) Acceptance or "positive submission." The hospice movement, which has helped many thousands of dying patients and their survivors, grew tremendously as a result of her work.

The New York Times went on to say, "Dr. Kübler-Ross was credited with helping end centuries-old taboos in Western culture against openly discussing and studying death. She also helped change the care of many terminally ill patients to make death less psychologically painful, not only for the dying, but also for their doctors and nurses—and not least for the survivors."

Just about everywhere you turn, you can read about the good work she did.

And yet, later in her career she became deeply involved in spiritism, talking openly about the "spirit guides" who mentored her. She said that guardian angels were actually spirit guides, as were children's imaginary playmates.

She explained that spirit guides are "people who have once lived in our physical world and then have died. Then they decide to help a person during his physical existence."

In 1977, she helped create a "healing center" in the mountains near Escondido, California. She spoke of staying up late into the night, talking and laughing with her spirit guides. She even said that one of her guides—a male named "Salem"—materialized and told her and the other members of her group that they had been together with Yeshua in Jerusalem 2,000 years ago. Kübler-Ross explained that the spirit guides actually took molecules out of a "spiritualist healer" named Jay Barham to clone a human being, and that's how they appeared. On one occasion a spirit guide named Mario had materialized from the waist up and had given her a back rub for 15 minutes.

The problem was that other members of Kübler-Ross's healing group disputed the appearance of "spirit guides." They alleged that what was really happening was that Barham was running around disguised as "a spirit entity," and said that he had lured some female members of the group into having sex with him by pretending to be the spirits of their dead husband.

The San Diego County district attorney's office even came to the healing center to investigate the alleged molestation of a 10-year-old girl by a "spirit entity"—but declined to press charges due to a lack of evidence. What a mess![1]

And yet Kübler-Ross stood by her friend the medium, whom she said was a man of unquestioned integrity. Using a metaphor straight from the Bible, she said, "Many attempts have been made to discredit us. To respond to them would be like casting pearls to swine" (see Matthew 7:6).

Elisabeth Kübler-Ross was regarded by many as a brilliant woman. But she was completely fooled by the charlatan Jay Barham and her relationship with her "spirit guides"—which I believe were demons. Her credibility was seriously damaged, and her marriage of 21 years broke up. Her story is a cautionary tale about what happens to those who become so obsessed about what happens on "the other side" that they lose their perspective and good judgment.

I believe it's a good thing to spend some time reflecting about the life beyond this one. But there is a line that should not be crossed.

SEPARATION FROM GOD

Although often disguised in the terminology of death, darkness, the underworld, and the grave, Jewish thought has, for centuries, acknowledged the existence of a place of separation from God and His blessings. Consider these passages:

- Deuteronomy 32:22 (NIV): "For a fire will be kindled by my wrath, one that burns down to the realm of the dead below...."

- 2 Samuel 22:6 (KJV): "The sorrows of hell compassed me about; the snares of death prevented me...."

- Job 11:8 (KJV): "It is as high as heaven; what canst thou do? Deeper than hell; what canst thou know?"

- Psalm 9:17 (KJV): "The wicked shall be turned into hell, and all the nations that forget God."

- Psalm 55:15 (KJV): "Let death seize upon them, and let them go down quick into hell: for wickedness is in their dwellings, and among them."

- Proverbs 7:27 (KJV): "Her house is the way to hell, going down to the chambers of death."

- Isaiah 14:15 (NIV): "But you are brought down to the realm of the dead, to the depths of the pit."

- Daniel 12:2 (NIV): "Multitudes who sleep in the dust of the earth will awake: some to everlasting life, others to shame and everlasting contempt."

From this small sampling of representative Old Testament passages, it is evident that Jewish cosmology had a complete and explicit view of hell, both its reality and its purpose in God's divine plan. That view changed with time, as Jewish doctrine came under the influence of secular humanism and moved away from its Orthodox roots.

THE VALLEY OF SLAUGHTER

The term *Gehenna* is a particularly fascinating variant for hell in Jewish literature. It is frequently found in the apocalyptic books that were written from 200 B.C. to A.D. 100, between the completion of the Old Testament and canon of the New Testament. With the exception of a single reference in the book of James, Gehenna is spoken of in Scripture only by Yeshua Himself. The Messiah was aware of the extraordinary significance of the term to His Jewish listeners and made compelling use of it in His teachings.

Gehenna refers directly to the Valley of Hinnom, just south of Jerusalem. The Bible first mentions it in the book of Joshua, where it is defined as the boundary between the tribes of Judah and Benjamin. During the second temple period (500 B.C.–A.D. 70), the valley was a vast garbage dump, with piles of refuse burning day and night.

But Gehenna had an even more sinister connotation. In ancient times, parents had sacrificed their children to the loathsome Canaanite god Molech (also called Molek) here. The altars of Molech were subsequently destroyed by Josiah, as recorded in 2 Kings 23:10. But the horrifying rituals practiced in Hinnom lived on in the imagination of Jerusalem's population. The prophet Jeremiah described the locale as a "Valley of Slaughter" (Jeremiah 19:6).

It was subsequently used as a burial ground for criminals before it became the city's trash dump.

Over time, Gehenna came to be synonymous with hell—a place where the wicked dead are punished in fire that is sixty times hotter than ordinary fire.[2] According to one teaching in the Talmud, souls consigned to Gehenna would first be afflicted with terrible itching. Then they would be burned with fire. After that, they would endure terrible cold and snow.[3]

Simcha Paull Raphael writes, "The idea of a world of postmortem punishment was very real to the Rabbis and their disciples. They saw Gehenna as an abode of punishment for the person who did not live a righteous life in accordance with the ways of God and the Torah (Exodus Rabbah 2:2). That belief was central to their daily lives."[4]

Some sages believed that Gehenna was a place of rehabilitation. Souls were purified there until they were ready to spend eternity in God's presence. Some taught that even those who had arrived at the gates of Gehenna could still repent, receive divine mercy, and be spared from punishment.[5]

The apocryphal book of 3 Enoch, which has been traced as far back as the fifth century, elaborates on this:

> The souls of the wicked are brought down to Sheol
> by two angels of destruction, Zaapiel and Samkiel.
> Samkiel is in charge of the souls of the intermediate,
> to support them and purify them from sin through
> the abundant mercies of the Omnipotent One.
> Zaapiel is appointed to bring down the souls of the
> wicked from the presence of the Holy One, blessed
> be he, from the judgment of the Shechina to Sheol

to punish them with fire in Gahinnom with rods of burning coal.[6]

The great Jewish scholar Shammai (50 B.C.–A.D. 30), who lived during the time of Yeshua, said:

> There will be three groups on the Day of Judgment: one of thoroughly righteous people, one of thoroughly wicked people, and one of people in between. The first group will be inscribed for everlasting life; the second group will be doomed in Gehinnom [forever]…the third will go down to Gehinnom and squeal and rise again [to be healed].[7]

The more tolerant school of Hillel (110 B.C. to A.D. 10), argued that God would be merciful, give those "in between" the benefit of the doubt, and thus send them to paradise rather than to Gehenna on the Day of Judgment. Another ancient sage from that period, Hanina, taught that all who go down to hell will go up again, except the following: the adulterer, one who puts his fellow to shame in public, and one who calls his fellow by an obnoxious nickname.[8]

Hillel and Shammai were contemporaries who founded opposing schools of thought. In the Talmud alone, more than 300 issues are debated by adherents of both schools. For instance, the House of Hillel taught that study of the Torah should be open to everyone, whereas the House of Shammai taught only to those who had shown themselves worthy.

Other differences between the two schools: Shammai taught that it was always a sin to tell a lie, even if was to prevent hurt feelings—such as telling a homely bride that she looks beautiful. Hillel countered that all brides are beautiful on their wedding day. The

House of Shammai said that a man could divorce his wife only for a serious transgression, whereas the House of Hillel allowed divorce for almost any offense, even a burned dinner. The two houses also differed in their opinion of how Hanukkah was to be observed. The House of Hillel taught that one candle should be lighted on the first night and another added each night until eight candles were burning. The House of Shammai taught that eight candles should be lighted on the first night and then one extinguished each night after that.

Such matters may seem trivial, but followers of Hillel and Shammai took them very seriously—as they did their opinions about what happens to the human soul after death.

A story in Shabbat 31a of the Talmud humorously shows the difference in personality and approach between the two famous rabbis. The story concerns a Gentile who said he wanted to convert to Judaism, but only if a rabbi would teach him the entire Torah while he stood on one foot. First he went to Shammai who was insulted by the man's preposterous request and threw him out of his house. Then he went to Hillel. Hillel accepted the challenge. As the fellow stood on one foot, the rabbi told him, "What is hateful to you, do not do to your neighbor. That is the whole Torah; the rest is the explanation of this—go and study it!"

Some scholars suggest Yeshua Himself may have known this story. If so, He turned it upside down and gave it a more positive, proactive spin in the Golden Rule: "So in everything, do to others what you would have them do to you, for this sums up the Law and the Prophets" (Matthew 7:12).

Simcha Paull Raphael writes, "The Rabbis often discuss the duration of punishment in Gehenna. The generally accepted belief was that the punitive tortures of Gehenna are time-limited, not eternal. Eternal punishment was never accepted as a doctrinal belief in Rabbinic Judaism."[9] The tractate Shabbat says clearly that "the punishment of the dead in Gehenna is twelve months."[10]

Others took the view that although many souls would be purged of their wickedness in Gehenna, others were so consumed with wickedness that they could never be purified. These souls would be burned and their ashes scattered.

The apocryphal book of 1 Enoch, which has been dated to the early first century, had much to say about the punishment that awaits evildoers in the next life:

> And behold, they were all bound, I saw, and they all stood before Him. And the judgment was held and they were judged and found guilty, and went to the place of condemnation, and they were cast into an abyss, full of fire and flaming, full of pillars of fire (1 Enoch 90:23-26).

> In those days, Sheol shall open its jaws. And they will be swallowed up therein, and their destruction will be at an end; Sheol will devour the sinners in the presence of the elect" (1 Enoch 56:8).

> Know that their souls will descend into Sheol, and they will be wretched in their great tribulation. And into darkness and chains and a burning flame where there is grievous judgment shall your spirits enter; and the great judgment shall be for all the generations of

the world. Woe to you, for you shall have no peace"
(1 Enoch 63:1).

In the Tractate Gehinnom, the sages describe with vivid clarity the punishments that will be inflicted on the wicked dead. (*Gehenna* is the Greek name of the place where the dead are punished. *Gehinnom* is the Hebrew name.)

Simcha Paull Raphael says that in this tractate: "Individual senses and body parts are tortured in retribution for moral transgressions involving such senses, limbs, genitals, breasts, hair and so on." He admits that some of the tortures may seem cruel to the modern hearer, but quotes Saul Lieberman who says that "some of the cruel punishments used by the Roman authorities were inserted into Gehenna from real practice, and the authors were speaking of the ordinary custom."[11]

The Tractate Gehinnom teaches that there are burning coals in Gehenna that are as large as the Dead Sea, and rivers of pitch and sulfur "flowing and fuming and seething."[12] The tractate also says, "The punishment of the sinner is this: the angels of destruction throw him to the flame of Gehinnom, and this opens its mouth wide and swallows him. This all happens to him who has not done one single pious act that would incline the balance toward mercy."[13]

Rabbi Yohanan writes that those who are sent to Gehenna have "a body that is never destroyed and whose soul enters a fire that is never extinguished...." Still, the prevailing view seems to be that the punishment will last a maximum of 12 months—after which some say the wicked will be destroyed and their ashes scattered, and others believe they will be purified and rise to paradise, known as Gan Eden (the Garden of Eden).[14]

Another Rabbi, Joshua ben Levi, tells of being taken to the gates of Gehenna by the prophet Elijah. Here he sees men hanging by their hair. "These were the men that let their hair grow to adorn themselves for sin." Others are hanging by their eyes because they followed their eyes to sin "and did not set the Holy Blessed One before them." Still others hang by their noses because they "perfumed themselves to sin," or by their feet because "they had run to sin." He tells of those who had blasphemed being fed fiery coals, and some being thrown from fire to snow and then back to snow because they had abused the poor who had come to them for help.[15]

Rabbi Yohanan says:

> For every sin there is an angel appointed to obtain the expiation thereof; one comes first and obtains his expiation, then follows another and so on until all the sins are expiated. As with a debtor who has many creditors, and come before the king to claim their debts, and the king delivers him to them and says, "Take him and divide him between yourselves," so also is the soul delivered in Gehinnom to cruel angels and they divide it among themselves.[16]

In the Kabbalah, the mystic teachings of the Jewish sages, Gehenna is described as a "waiting room" or "entryway" for the souls of the dead. According to these writings, it was not a permanent place of punishment, but rather a sort of "spiritual forge" where one became aware of the sins committed in life. The rabbis taught that the longest a soul could dwell in Gehenna was one year, before ascending to a purified state.

GEHENNA IN THE TEACHINGS OF YESHUA

Yeshua clearly saw it in completely different terms. He most definitely saw it as a place of eternal punishment. He taught extensively about hell (Gehenna), bringing clarity to a subject that thus far in rabbinic teaching may have been somewhat ambiguous.

> *If your right eye causes you to stumble, gouge it out and throw it away! It is better for you that one part of your body should be destroyed, than that your whole body be thrown into Gehenna. And if your right hand causes you to stumble, cut it off and throw it away! It is better for you that one part of your body should be destroyed than that your whole body to go into Gehenna* (Matthew 5:29-30).

A few chapters later, Yeshua tells His followers not to be afraid of what kills the body, but rather, *"do not fear those who kill the body...Instead, fear the One who is able to destroy both soul and body in Gehenna"* (Matthew 10:28).

Like all good Jewish storytellers, Yeshua placed great value on the resonant metaphor. Gehenna, with its all its ghastly and accursed connotations, was a perfect picture of hell: a place devoid of hope, filled with tormented souls and unfit for habitation by those who love God and feared His commandments. When He used the word to evoke hell and all its terrors, the Messiah was tapping in to a deep vein of Jewish belief. To the ancient Jewish mind, hell was far more than a theological abstraction. It was, in every sense of the word, a *real* place.

Chapter 8

The Christian View of Hell

From the early days of Christianity, most Christian scholars and theologians have thought of hell as a real place of punishment, reserved for evildoers and those who reject the grace of God.

Not all Christian denominations believe in hell, however. Seventh-Day Adventists don't believe that hell currently exists, or that hell is a place of eternal punishment. They believe, instead, that the dead will merely sleep until the resurrection at the end of the world, when all the wicked will be destroyed.

But almost all others have historically believed in the hell of everlasting fire that Jesus talks about in the New Testament. On July 16, 2014, the Southern Baptist Convention voted to affirm its stance that hell is a place of "conscious, eternal punishment" for those who don't accept God's plan of salvation as offered in the New Testament Scriptures.

According to the Religious News Service, the vote came as a response to *Love Wins,* a book by Michigan Pastor Rob Bell that questions traditional views of hell. "Citing Bell's book, 'Love Wins,' the resolution urges Southern Baptists 'to proclaim faithfully the depth and gravity of sin against a holy God, the reality of hell, and the salvation of sinners by God's grace alone, through faith alone, in Jesus Christ [Messiah] alone, to the glory of God alone."

Despite the controversy that rages today regarding hell's existence, the early fathers of the Christian church clearly taught that hell is real.

About 120 years after Yeshua's death, Justin Martyr wrote:

> Every man will receive the eternal punishment or reward which his actions deserve. Indeed, if all men recognized this, no one would choose evil even for a short time, knowing that he would incur the eternal sentence of fire. On the contrary, he would take every means to control himself and to adorn himself in virtue, so that he might obtain the good gifts of God and escape the punishments.[1]

Thirty years later, Theophilus of Antioch warned:

> For the unbelievers and for the contemptuous and for those who do not submit to the truth but assent to iniquity, when they have been involved in adulteries, and fornications, and homosexualities, and avarice, and in lawless idolatries, there will be wrath and indignation, tribulation and anguish; and in the end, such men as these will be detained in everlasting fire.[2]

In A.D. 212, Hippolytus wrote of the unquenchable and unending fire that awaits the wicked, along with "a certain fiery worm which does not die and which does not waste the body but continually bursts forth from the body with unceasing pain. No sleep will give them rest; no night will soothe them; no death will deliver them from punishment; no appeal of interceding friends will profit them."[3]

We can see from these writings, and many others, that the leaders of the early Christian church believed that hell was real and that it was a place of everlasting torment reserved for sinners who had turned their backs on the grace of God.

The Apostles' Creed, which can be traced back as far as the fourth century, says that Yeshua "descended into hell" after His death.

The New Testament book of 1 Peter seems to refer to this when it says, "For the Messiah also suffered once for sins, the righteous for the unrighteous, to bring you to God. He was put to death in the body but made alive in the Spirit. After being made alive, he went and made proclamation to the imprisoned spirits—to those who were disobedient long ago when God waited patiently in the days of Noah while the ark was being built..." (1 Peter 3:18-20 NIV). First Peter 4:6 (NIV) adds that, "the gospel was preached even to those who are now dead, so that they might be judged according to human standards in regard to the body, but live according to God in regard to the spirit."

This is all the Bible says on the matter. Some argue that Yeshua did not descend into hell itself, but rather into the realm of the dead.

But in his book *Christ Alone,* Michael E. Wittmer writes:

We may not know why God does not save everyone from going to Hell, but we do know that God himself experienced it. The Apostles' Creed states that Jesus descended into Hell or "descended to the dead." In that eternal moment, when the perfect Son was intolerably forsaken by his Father, God himself experienced the worst torments of Hell. This does not tell us why God permits Hell to exist, but it does assure us that God is love. He may not get everyone out of Hell, but for our sake he has allowed Hell to get to him. No one will ever suffer more than our loving, infinite God already has. We may rightly wonder why God doesn't empty Hell, but we should never raise the question of Hell without shuddering even more at the thought of the cross.[4]

The existence of hell is under attack from many sides these days. Rob Bell isn't the only well-known or well-intentioned pastor who denies the existence of a place of eternal punishment.

The late theologian Clark Pinnock wrote:

Obviously, I am rejecting the traditional view of hell in part out of a sense of moral and theological revulsion to it. The idea that a conscious creature should have to undergo physical and mental torture through unending times is profoundly disturbing, and the thought that this is inflicted upon them by divine decree offends my conviction about God's love. This is probably the primary reason why people question the tradition so vehemently in the first place. They are not first of all impressed by its lack of a good scriptural basis (that comes later) but are appalled by its awful moral implications.[5]

I can certainly relate to Pinnock's moral and theological revulsion to a place so horrible existing in light of a loving God. It *is* profoundly disturbing. Keep in mind, however, our immediate tendency to be repelled by such a horrific idea comes from our limited, finite thinking. We cannot reconcile the idea of a loving God allowing such punishment upon anyone, except perhaps the most evil of humans. God is infinite however, and in that realm, we will perceive and think differently about things. In the realm of the infinite, things we do not understand here will make complete sense, including the existence of hell. As Paul tells us in 1 Corinthians, "For now we see in a mirror dimly, but then face to face. Now I know in part, but then I will know fully, even as have been fully known" (1 Corinthians 13:12).

In his later years, Anglican and Evangelical leader John Stott wrote:

> Emotionally, I find the concept [of eternal conscious torment] intolerable and do not understand how people can live with it without either cauterizing their feelings or cracking under the strain. But our emotions are a fluctuating, unreliable guide to truth and must not be exalted to the place of supreme authority in determining it…my question must be—and is—not what does my heart tell me, but what does God's word say?

> He urged that "the ultimate annihilation of the wicked should at least be accepted as a legitimate, biblically founded alternative to their eternal conscious torment.[6]

In her book *The Irrational Season,* Christian author Madeleine L'Engle wrote of her belief that:

> No matter how many eons it takes he (God) will not rest until all of creation, including Satan, is reconciled to him, until there is no creature who cannot return his look of love with a joyful response of love.... I cannot believe that God wants punishment to go on interminably any more than does a loving parent. The entire purpose of loving punishment is to teach, and it lasts only as long as it is needed for the lesson. And the lesson is always love.[7]

Even the Roman Catholic Church has changed its position on hell. In 1999, during the General Audience at the Vatican, Pope John Paul II changed the definition of hell to remove all threat of eternal torment. "Hell is not a punishment imposed externally by God, but the condition resulting from attitudes and actions which people adopt in this life," he said.

R. Albert Mohler Jr. writes:

> With this single sentence, the Pope denied that God imposes hell as a punishment and insisted that hell is now merely a "condition." He continued by explaining that "more than a physical place, hell is the state of those who freely and definitely separate themselves from God, the source of all life and joy. So eternal judgment is not God's work but is actually our own doing."
>
> Some conservative Catholics were unmoved. As an Australian priest opined, "Because Hell is not popular these days we cannot conclude that it is not populated.

If Dante were to visit hell in a new poetic reverie, would he find it closed up and boarded over?"[8]

Just a few years earlier in 1995, the Church of England Doctrine Commission released an official report titled "The Mystery of Salvation." The report, which was commissioned by the House of Bishops, stressed a hope for universal salvation, saying that it is "incompatible with the essential Christian affirmation that God is love to say that God brings millions into the world to damn them."[9]

And yet, as theologian J.I. Packer, author of *Knowing God*, points out:

> Universalists [those who think that everyone will eventually go to heaven] seem not to understand sin. Leaving Scripture behind, they second-guess God's plan by contending that he uses Hell to get sinners on track at last, and in so doing they fail to take the measure of the tragic twisting and shattering and consequent perversity of our souls through the Fall, and of the tragic irrationality and inaneness of sin as the now radical ruling force in humanity's spiritual system.
>
> Bodily addictions such as pill-popping and heroin-shooting can, we know, defy all attempts at therapy; is there any reason to suppose that the habit of sin will be easier to talk its addicts out of, even when our loving God is doing the talking?[10]

In other words, despite the fact that it is God's will that "none should perish and all come to repentance," some will continue to reject His repeated efforts to convict them of sin and repent, thus determining their eternal fate. (See 2 Peter 3:9.)

The New Testament gives some terrifying descriptions of hell—many of them from Yeshua Himself. According to these Scriptures, hell is:

- A place of weeping and gnashing of teeth: "Throw the worthless servant out, into the darkness where there will be weeping and gnashing of teeth" (Matthew 25:30).

- A place of outer darkness: "Then the king said to his servants, 'Tie him hand and foot, and throw him into the outer darkness; in that place will be weeping and gnashing of teeth'" (Matthew 22:13).

- A place of torment: "And from Sheol, as he was in torment, he raised his eyes. And he sees Abraham far off, with Lazarus at his side" (Luke 16:23).

- A place of everlasting destruction: "They will pay the price of eternal ruin, away from the presence of the Lord and the glory of His power" (2 Thessalonians 1:9).

- A place where the condemned are tormented with burning sulfur: "But for the cowardly and faithless and detestable and murderers and sexually immoral and sorcerers and idolaters and all liars—their lot is in the lake that burns with fire and brimstone, which is the second death" (Revelation 21:8).

- A place where the fire never goes out: "If your hand causes you to stumble, cut it off! It is better for you to enter life crippled than having two hands to go into Gehenna, into the unquenchable fire" (Mark 9:43).

- A bottomless pit: "And he opened the bottomless pit; and there arose a smoke out of the pit, as the smoke of a great furnace; and the sun and the air were darkened by reason of the smoke of the pit" (Revelation 9:2 KJV). The New International Version uses the word "abyss" in place of "bottomless pit."

- A place of no rest: "The smoke of their torment goes up forever and ever. Those who worship the beast and its image and those who receive the mark of his name have no rest day or night" (Revelation 14:11).

- A lake of fire (after the Final Judgment): "Then death and Sheol were thrown into the lake of fire. This is the second death—the lake of fire" (Revelation 20:14).

- A place of agony: "So he cried out and said, 'Father Abraham, have mercy on me! And send Lazarus so he may dip the tip of his finger in water and cool off my tongue, because I am suffering torment in this flame'" (Luke 16:24).

Why do people in the 21st century have such trouble believing in a place called hell, when human beings have acknowledged its existence for hundreds of years? Some say that belief in hell began to wane during World War I, when so many were suffering so terribly, especially in Europe. It seemed that hell had come to earth. So perhaps people stopped believing there could be more suffering in the afterlife, for anyone.

In 1741, American preacher and philosopher Jonathan Edwards delivered his well-known sermon, "Sinners in the Hands of an Angry God." Edwards pulled no punches in his description of hell, because he believed that hell is real, and he wanted his listeners to be warned so they wouldn't go there. Edwards told them:

> The God that holds you over the pit of hell, much as one holds a spider, or some loathsome insect, over the fire, abhors you, and is dreadfully provoked: his wrath towards you burns like fire; he looks upon you as worthy of nothing else, but to be cast into the fire; he is of purer eyes than to bear to have you in his sight; you are ten thousand times more abominable in his eyes as the most hateful venomous serpent is in ours. You have offended him infinitely more than ever a stubborn rebel did his prince; and yet it is nothing but his hand that holds you from falling into the fire every moment. It is to be ascribed to nothing else that you did not go to hell the last night; that you was suffered to awake again in this world, after you closed your eyes to sleep. And there is no other reason to be given, why you have not dropped into hell since you arose in the morning, but that God's hand has held you up. There is no other reason to be given why you have not gone to hell since you have sat here in the house of God, provoking his pure eyes by your sinful, wicked manner of attending his solemn worship. Yea there is nothing

else to be given as a reason why you do not this very
moment drop down into hell.[11]

Edwards continued by telling his congregation that God "will
crush you under his feet without mercy; he'll crush out your blood,
and make it fly, and it shall be sprinkled on his garments, so as to
stain all his raiment."[12]

Edwards' preaching helped ignite one of the greatest religious
revivals in American history. Yet today, I wonder how many would
even be willing to sit through such a sermon, or at least come away
deeply offended. Such a preacher would be branded as a hateful
fanatic. Even if people believe in hell, they don't want to hear about it.

And yet, if any period in the world's history has revealed the
evil depths of man's heart, it has been the past 100 years. When
I think about all the terrible and hellish things people have done
to each other, it makes me think that hell must exist. It has to, if
God is just—and I know He is. And paradise wouldn't be paradise
for very long if it was full of wicked and depraved people. Can you
imagine Adolf Hitler, Joseph Stalin, Idi Amin, or Osama bin Laden
in heaven? I certainly can't.

As I write this book, thousands of Iraqi Christians are being
slaughtered by a barbaric group of Muslim extremists known as
ISIS (Islamic State of Iraq and Syria). They have committed terrible atrocities, including beheading innocent children. Another
terrorist organization, Hamas, has fired over 3,000 rockets into
Israel, seeking to kill as many civilians as they can. And think of
all the people who suffered and died when Osama bin Laden and
Al-Qaeda attacked the World Trade Center on 9/11/2001.

Drug cartels in Mexico have murdered thousands upon thousands of people, including many unarmed civilians who were

slaughtered for no apparent reason. In North Korea, Kim Jong-un seems determined to outdo the depravity of his father.

And then I think about some of the other evils we've experienced in the past 100 years: six million Jews exterminated by Adolf Hitler and the Nazis. Millions more murdered by Mao Tse-tung in China and Joseph Stalin in Russia. Pol Pot and the Khmer Rouge in Cambodia. Genocide in Rwanda. The list goes on and on. Just pick up a newspaper or watch the news, and you'll quickly see the evil to which human beings can sink.

I look around and wonder if we haven't returned to the days before Noah and the Great Flood, when, "The Lord saw how great the wickedness of the human race had become on the earth, and that every inclination of the thoughts of the human heart was only evil all the time" (Genesis 6:5 NIV).

As we've already seen, Yeshua clearly taught that hell is a real place. In Matthew 5:22, He says, "I tell you now that everyone who is angry with his brother [or sister] shall be subject to judgment. And whoever says to his brother [or sister], 'Raca,' shall be subject to the council; and whoever says, 'You fool!' shall be subject to fiery Gehenna."

Again and again, Yeshua drives home the point: hell is a real place—the sorrowful destination of those who have rejected God's mercy—and it is better to lose everything in this life than to risk ending up there for eternity.

The Bible is also clear that God holds individuals accountable for their decision in this life to believe or reject the truth of His existence. Romans chapter 1 tells us that:

> *The wrath of God is being revealed from heaven against all the godlessness and unrighteousness of men. In unrighteousness they suppress the truth, because what*

can be known about God is plain to them—for God has shown it to them. His invisible attributes—His eternal power and His divine nature—have been clearly seen ever since the creation of the world, being understood through the things that have been made. So people are without excuse (Romans 1:18-20).

Yeshua was also critical of those who, because of their pride and arrogance, rejected God's truth. We see this in His fiery rebuke of Capernaum:

Woe to you, Chorazin! Woe to you, Bethsaida! For if the miracles done in you had been done in Tyre and Sidon, they would have turned [repented] long ago, sitting in sackcloth and ashes. Yet it will be more bearable for Tyre and Sidon at the Judgment than for you! And you, Capernaum? You won't be lifted to heaven, will you? No, you will go down as far as Sheol (Luke 10:13-15).

He also issued a direct and pointed warning to His followers: "I will show you whom you should fear. Fear the One who, after the killing, has authority to cast into Gehenna. Yes, I tell you, fear this One!" (Luke 12:5).

THE RICH MAN AND LAZARUS

One of the clearest revelations we find in the New Testament about hell is found in chapter 16 of Luke, where Yeshua relates the parable of the Rich Man and Lazarus. Perhaps I should explain that most biblical scholars believe the story to be a parable, although the Bible doesn't really say.

In almost all other instances when Jesus was teaching through use of parables, the Bible explains that this is so. But in the case of the Rich Man and Lazarus, Yeshua launches right into the story with the words, "There was a certain rich man…" Could it be that He's telling about something that actually happened? Whether this is the case or not we can't say, but Luke 16:19-31 (NIV) tells a compelling story:

> There was a rich man who was dressed in purple and fine linen and lived in luxury every day. At his gate was laid a beggar named Lazarus, covered with sores and longing to eat what fell from the rich man's table. Even the dogs came and licked his sores.
>
> The time came when the beggar died and the angels carried him to Abraham's side. The rich man also died and was buried. In Hades, where he was in torment, he looked up and saw Abraham far away, with Lazarus by his side. So he called to him, "Father Abraham, have pity on me and send Lazarus to dip the tip of his finger in water and cool my tongue, because I am in agony in this fire."
>
> But Abraham replied, "Son, remember that in your lifetime you received your good things, while Lazarus received bad things, but now he is comforted here and you are in agony. And besides all this, between us and you a great chasm has been set in place, so that those who want to go from here to you cannot, nor can anyone cross over from there to us."

He answered, "Then I beg you, father, send Lazarus to my family, for I have five brothers. Let him warn them, so that they will not also come to this place of torment."

Abraham replied, "They have Moses and the Prophets; let them listen to them."

"No, father Abraham," he said, "but if someone from the dead goes to them, they will repent."

He said to him, "If they do not listen to Moses and the Prophets, they will not be convinced even if someone rises from the dead."

Obviously, there are several important truths to be learned from this passage.

1. The way we treat "the least of these" is extremely important. (See Matthew 25:31-46; Isaiah 58:7.) The rich man was not concerned about those who were poor and suffering. He did not heed the commandment of God to "love your neighbor as yourself" (Leviticus 19:18; Matthew 22:39), and now he was paying a high price for his callous and indifferent lifestyle.

2. Earthly rewards lose their value in the face of death. The rich man had all he needed and more in this world. It was all taken from him at the moment of death. Sumptuous riches and lavish spending were replaced by an eternity of suffering. Someone once said, "I've never see a hearse towing a U-Haul." We

came into the world with nothing and we will leave the world with nothing. Yeshua provided sound advice when He warned us, "Do not store up for yourselves treasures on earth, where moth and rust destroy and where thieves break in and steal. But store up for yourselves treasures in heaven, where neither moth nor rust destroys and where thieves do not break in or steal. For where your treasure is, there will your heart be also" (Matthew 6:19-21). What you do with the money God has entrusted to you will show where your heart really is.

3.   Some who suffer on earth will reap great rewards in heaven. Lazarus had no reward on earth. His treasure was in heaven, symbolized here by that metaphor of returning to the ancestors, "the bosom of Abraham," a widely recognized image of paradise. You may be going through great challenges in this life. All may appear hopeless. You may even feel like you are living in a hell on earth. Just remember, if you put your trust in the Lord, the riches that lay ahead for you will make up for everything you may be going through now. (Read Romans 8:17-18.)

4.   Hell is real, and whether or not we end up there after we die depends on the decisions we make in this life. The rich man even begs Abraham to send Lazarus to his five living brothers to warn them what awaits those who spurn God's law and refuse to show His love and mercy to the poor. Abraham responds that his brothers have the witness of Moses and all the prophets as

a warning to live according to the commandments of God. If they did not heed these authoritative voices, Abraham declares, they will not heed the voice of Lazarus, even though he returned from the dead.

HELL: A COMMON THEME

As Christopher Morgan points out, "the future punishment of the wicked in hell is a significant theme in the New Testament." He adds that all New Testament authors—Matthew, Mark, Luke, John, Paul, James, Peter, Jude, and the author of Hebrews—refer to hell in some way. Taking all of these various Scriptures into account, Morgan says that an interesting thing to note is that overall each New Testament writer's descriptions closely resemble those of the others.[13]

Combining the various teachings on hell, Morgan comes up with three "predominant pictures of hell":

1. Hell is a place of punishment: "The chief description of hell in the New Testament is punishment."

2. Hell is a place of destruction: Morgan quotes Matthew 7:13-14 (NIV), among numerous other passages. "Enter through the narrow gate. For wide is the gate and broad is the road that leads to destruction, and many enter through it. But small is the gate and narrow the road that leads to life, and only a few find it."

3. Hell is a place of banishment: The New Testament teaches that souls in hell are "cut off" from God, and Morgan interprets this to mean that they have

been banished from God's presence. "Banishment is much stronger than separation," Morgan writes. "It suggests God's active judgment while separation could simply imply divine passivity. Banishment also stresses the dreadfulness and finality of the predicament."[14]

In the book of Revelation, the apostle John uses sweeping, cinematic language to discuss the nature and purpose of hell:

The sea gave up the dead that were in it, and death and Sheol gave up the dead that were in them. Then they were each judged, each one of them, according to their deeds. Then death and Sheol were thrown into the lake of fire. This is the second death—the lake of fire. And if anyone was not found written in the Book of Life, he was thrown into the lake of fire (Revelation 20:13-15).

Although this passage is quite complex and parts of it are an enigma and open to various interpretations, some of the language is crystal clear. There *will* be a future judgment for every person who has ever lived and *only those written in the "Book of Life"* will escape this final punishment. Frightening and sobering words to ponder, to say the least.

I remember reciting a prayer each year at Yom Kippur (the Day of Atonement) in synagogue all through my childhood years that basically asked the Lord to remember us and inscribe us in the book of life. I always wondered if my name was written in the book. Now I know that it is. What about you? Do you know for certain that your name is written in the book of life? You can.

Yeshua the Messiah declared, "...I am the First and the Last, and the One who lives. I was dead, but look—I am alive forever and ever! Moreover, I hold the keys of death and Sheol" (Revelation 1:17-18).

Yeshua alone holds those keys and He alone provides the way into heaven, for "there is salvation in *no* one else, for there is *no other name* under heaven given to mankind by which we must be saved" (Acts 4:12).

Part Four

THOSE WHO HAVE GONE
BEYOND THE VEIL

Chapter 9

VOICES FROM THE OTHER SIDE

I'VE NEVER HAD A Near-Death Experience. But I believe they happen. I believe because I've talked to men and women who've had them.

I've seen looks of terror come across the faces of people as they remember the excruciating tortures they encountered in hell. I've heard the unmistakable urgency in their voices when they've told me, "I don't ever want to go back there."

I've also seen a joyful sparkle come into people's eyes as they told me about the joys they encountered in heaven. I've heard the wistful, yearning tone in people's voices that says, "I can't wait to go back there."

As I mentioned previously, in preparing to write this book, I spent more than a year checking out Near-Death Experiences.

With the help of a full-time researcher, we read or skimmed through numerous books on the subject. We also plowed through dozens of news articles. The books and the articles ranged from the ridiculous to the sublime. Yes, there were some who seemed anxious to cash in on a good thing. Near-Death Experiences sold books, so they had Near-Death Experiences.

But many others were not like that. When they described what had happened to them, it rang true. I'm not a gullible guy. I strive to be open-minded, but I definitely don't believe everything I hear. I'm not easily scammed, and I have a pretty good sense of when someone is trying to sell me a bill of goods. But as I read these people's accounts of their journeys to the other side, there was a feeling deep down inside of me that they were telling the truth. It was similar to what happened to me as a college student, when I was confronted with the gospel at a home Bible study. I just knew in my heart that there was a God and that I was separated from Him because of my sin. My mind may have been fighting, but I knew in my heart it was true.

I am not by any means trying to equate these Near-Death stories with the authority of the Bible. I do not base my faith in the reality of heaven or hell on any of these testimonies. Yes, there is some faith involved in believing their accounts. I did pray for discernment as I investigated these Near-Death stories, and I believe God led me.

I also looked for a lifestyle that is consistent with what these people say they have experienced. Are they living lives that tell me they truly know there is another life beyond this one, and that this life is merely preparation for what is to come? To put it more simply, I looked to see if their walk lines up with their talk. The ones I chose to pursue were those who demonstrated godly character and fruit in their lives.

The next step was to call the writers who had impressed me the most and interview them. Several of these were then invited to appear on our television show, *Jewish Voice with Jonathan Bernis*.

Frankly, it was not easy to pare down the stories. We interviewed many more people who experienced either visions of the afterlife, NDEs, or clinical deaths than I decided to write about in this book. With the exception of Bill Wiese, who experienced such a dramatic and graphic vision of hell that I felt I needed to include him, I chose to focus on those who actually died. Those I decided to include provided medical records to prove that they had, indeed, been pronounced dead. Some of the records I reviewed were quite extensive and showed massive injuries that were inoperable.

Two Types of Death

As Don Piper explained to me, there are two forms of death—clinical death and biological death. The difference between the two is a matter of minutes. Clinical death is the point at which a person's heart stops beating and the blood ceases to circulate. Biological death occurs four to six minutes later, when the brain can no longer function due to a lack of oxygen. One of the men I interviewed—Dr. Gary Wood—was dead for more than an hour. Don Piper was deceased for 90 minutes, and Dean Braxton for one hour and 45 minutes.

The people I talked to came from vastly different backgrounds. Some had been believers from childhood. Others were atheists or agnostics. One, Earthquake Kelley, had been deeply involved in drugs and Satan worship.

Interviewees included both men and women from various socio-economic backgrounds, ethnicities, and educational levels. While they all had unique stories about their upbringings and the events that had led to their encounters with death, most of them shared some significant things in common.

For example, the vast majority now had a strong, personal relationship with God. In every case, these people told me they experienced total peace, joy, and jubilation as they died. Or, if they died in accidents, as was the case with Don Piper and Dr. Gary Wood, they were immediately enveloped in an environment of peace and tranquility. This actually surprised a couple of them. They told me they had expected to experience some fear or apprehension. Instead, they were immediately bathed in bright light and surrounded by a peace that passed all understanding (see Philippians 4:7).

Exceptions to this included Howard Storm and Earthquake Kelley, who experienced great fear and dread as he was dragged down to hell by demons when he died as a teenager. Brought back by the prayers of his believing mother, Kelley died again 36 years later, this time ending up in "the right place," and experiencing incredible peace and jubilation. Howard Storm told me that when he died, he knew he had "lived an unsatisfactory life," and that he had rejected the Lord his entire adult life. He was horrified as he realized that he had died and was utterly without an excuse for the way he had lived. He knew he deserved to be where he was—and he was not in heaven.

Meeting with Friends and Family

All of those who said they had gone to heaven told me they were met by friends and family there. The reunions occurred either inside the heavenly city, or at the gates of heaven. Many spoke of meeting departed relatives they had never met in this life—great grandmothers and grandfathers, for example—or people who had died very young, or as babies. Even though they had never met these relatives or hadn't seen them in many years, they recognized them immediately. There was no need for spoken introductions—the bond was so strong. Some told me that the ones who greeted them had all played some role in their spiritual pilgrimage. Gary Wood said that everyone is assigned someone to meet them and take them around heaven. Others reported an entire welcoming delegation.

Don Piper remembers meeting his grandfather, who had passed away from a heart attack. The elderly gentleman had lost some fingers in an industrial accident prior to his death, but in heaven, all his fingers had been restored. Earthquake Kelley was reunited with his son, who had been murdered six years previously. Gary Wood was delighted to see a college friend who had been decapitated in a horrible accident.

All the people who said they had been to heaven told me how great the people they saw looked. Everyone they met on the other side had perfect, beautiful bodies. No one was wrinkled, stooped, or looked old or unhealthy. Any lost body parts, deformities, or blemishes had been healed and restored. It seems that Yeshua alone is scarred in heaven—His hands and feet still bearing the nail scars that speak of His great love for us all.

NO ONE WANTED TO RETURN

Another common feeling expressed by all those who had been to heaven was that none of them wanted to come back to this world. None of them had thought about the loved ones they were leaving behind. None of them yearned to return to complete unfinished tasks. No one had feelings of regret that they had died too young, or had been cheated by an untimely death. Every one of them wanted to stay in heaven and were disappointed when told they couldn't.

Howard Storm referred to heaven as "the fun center of the universe," and told me that if people knew how great heaven really is, many fewer people would want to remain here on earth.

Perhaps the thing that I found most intriguing, in both my on-camera interviews and personal discussions over lunches and dinners, was that those who died and came back no longer feel at home here. They long for "another country" that awaits at the end of this life. I could hear the desire in their voices and see it in their eyes. They yearn to get back "home" as soon as they possibly can. But all of them understand that they came back for a reason, and that they have work to do here. Some came back to bodies that were damaged—even mangled—and experienced months or even years of pain. Some, like Don Piper, had to undergo numerous operations.

None came back because they wanted to. Rather, they had no choice. They came back to serve God. They came back to tell us about their experiences and to share their faith. They are warning us to get ready for the afterlife. They don't want us to be like the rich farmer in the parable found in chapter 12 of Luke:

> And Yeshua told them a parable, saying, "The land of a certain rich man produced good crops. And he began thinking to himself, saying, 'What shall I do? I don't have a place to store my harvest!' And he said, 'Here's what I'll do! I'll tear down my barns and build larger ones, and there I'll store all my grain and my goods. And I'll say to myself, "O my soul, you have plenty of goods saved up for many years! So take it easy! Eat, drink, and be merry."' But God said to him, 'You fool! Tonight your soul is being demanded back from you! And what

you have prepared, whose will that be?' So it is with the one who stores up treasure for himself and is not rich in God" (Luke 12:16-21).

Death is coming for us all. It is absolutely essential that we be ready to go.

THE IMPORTANCE OF WORSHIP

Another thing everyone agreed about was the importance and prominence of worship in heaven. I heard testimonies about thousands upon thousands of worshipers in heaven, all singing different songs that somehow managed to harmonize and all flow together. Don Piper told me that music "surrounded me and invaded me." Can you imagine? Thousands of songs rendered at the same time without chaos, interfacing together, glorifying God. The one song soaring over all the rest was "Holy, Holy, Holy." He told me he still hears this music today.

Many told me that every object in heaven is alive and worships God, including inanimate objects. Dean Braxton said that everything in heaven is alive—that nothing is dead there. Even the atmosphere is alive. Objects such as the altar and the throne of God are alive and worship Him. Flowers, trees, and grass all worship God. Even the rocks cry out in praise.

One thing I heard clearly from everyone: If you don't like to worship God you won't like heaven. So we'd better prepare now. Worship is one of the primary things we'll do in heaven—a way of life there.

The six testimonies I have chosen to share with you in this book are: Howard Storm, Don Piper, Bill Wiese, Dr. Gary L. Wood, Curtis "Earthquake" Kelley, and Dean Braxton.

Let's begin with Howard Storm. When we last saw Howard, he was in pitch-black darkness, swinging wildly, trying to fight off hordes of human-like creatures that were swarming over him, trying to tear him apart. They slashed at him with their long claws and fangs.

Five minutes previously, Howard Storm didn't believe in demons. But that was back on the other side—in the hospital room where his lifeless body lay...

Chapter 10

HOWARD STORM

LET ME BACK UP for a moment to explain how Howard Storm wound up in the darkness, fighting back against demons who were trying to tear him apart.

It was 1985. Howard Storm was 38 years of age, an art professor at Northern Kentucky University. "I believed that there was no God and that religion was hocus-pocus and superstition," he said. "I was a die-hard atheist, and quite vocal about it. I knew for a certainty that we were just biochemical, electrical entities, and when life ended, we ended. That was all there was to it."

Howard was in Paris, France, at the end of a three-week art tour through Europe, when he suddenly suffered a severe perforation of his duodenum. "It was the most intense pain I'd ever experienced, right in the center of my belly," he remembers. The pain was so intense, he fell to the ground, "kicking and screaming in terror."

Howard's colleagues called the desk at the hotel where they were staying and contacted medical services. A doctor quickly arrived, examined Howard, and announced that he had to have emergency surgery right away. An ambulance came shortly after that, and, with siren blaring and lights flashing, transported Howard to a hospital some eight miles away. Upon arrival at that hospital, he was again examined by two doctors who said he would be taken to a surgical center another few miles away. All this time, Howard Storm was moaning in pain. He would have prayed for relief, but he didn't believe there was anyone to pray to.

"It was made clear to both my wife and me that if I didn't have the surgery within an hour, I would die," Howard remembers. Later on, doctors in the United States told him that given the severity of his condition, five hours was the longest amount of time he could have been expected to survive without surgery.

Howard was rushed to the surgical center by the ambulance and deposited in a hospital bed. And then, apparently, simply forgotten. "They put me in a room and left me there for ten hours. No doctor, no nurse, no medical attention at all. It was the weekend, and most of the staff was gone. I just fell through the cracks of the system they had in place."

I searched Howard's face for signs of anger over what happened to him, but found none. As severe as the pain was, he believes now that everything that happened to him was preordained.

"I'm firmly convinced that I died while I was in the room," he told me. "Doctors in the United States later told me it was a miracle that I survived in that room for as long as I did, considering the size of the perforation in my stomach."

After a time, not being to deal with the pain any longer, Howard passed out. "I don't know how long I was unconscious, but when I finally woke up, the pain was gone. My first emotion was joy: somehow, miraculously, I had gotten better. I looked around and found myself standing next to the bed, and to my confusion and horror there was something in the bed that looked exactly like my body. Somehow I knew it was really was me, but at the same time, I knew I wasn't alive anymore. I can't emphasize how terrifying that realization was. This couldn't be happening."

HOWARD, HURRY, COME WITH US!

"The room was brightly lit and I heard people's voices calling my name. I went to the doorway and looked down the hallway. There were people standing there, shadowy and gray, and they were saying 'Howard, hurry, come with us. We can't wait any longer.' And I replied, 'I'm sick, I need a doctor. I need surgery.' And they were saying, 'We don't have time for this. We know all about you. We've been waiting a long time for you.'"

You already know what happened next. Howard followed the voices down the hall, thinking he was being led to surgery. But as the mysterious group moved forward, the hall became darker and the situation more mysterious and terrifying.

"It got darker and darker, and I became increasingly frightened just by being with them. I knew that this was not a good situation. I knew that, wherever I was, I was not in Paris, I was not in the hospital, and I wasn't going to surgery. At that point I understood something bad was happening. I finally told them I wasn't going with them any farther. The only problem was, I had no idea where I actually was. I was surrounded by complete, abject darkness, and

I didn't know which way to go. And the dark shadowy figures all around me insisted, 'You're almost there.'"

When Howard refused to go any farther, his companions began to push and pull at him. They called him vulgar names. They taunted him with comments that showed they knew his deepest secrets. When nothing else worked, they began hitting and clawing at him.

"I fought back as best I could," Howard said. "That only made them more violent and vicious, biting, scratching, and tearing at me. I was sure that this was all just the introduction to more horrible things they were going to do with me. The pain that they inflicted was terrible. I was being torn apart, bitten, and scratched to pieces."

Howard shudders at the memory. A shadow moves across his face—a look of sadness and regret.

"Later, when I went back and tried to make sense of what had happened to me, I came to the conclusion that I had led an unsatisfactory life. I felt that I not been a good son. I had not been a good father or teacher and had never been the great artist I thought I was going to be. I was a failure as a person. And I realized, and this is very hard for me to say, that these people were just like me. They had rejected God and everything about Him. The way I thought about it was that I had been flushed down the sewage system into the cesspool of the universe. The worst thing was that, deep down inside, I knew I belonged there. I had no excuse for the way I had lived my life. Now I was dead and this was my fate."

Howard was vastly outnumbered by the horde that tore and slashed at him. Just as he was about to give up, he heard a voice. "It sounded like my voice, but I wasn't speaking," he recalls. "Pray to God," the voice commanded. "But I don't believe in God," Howard thought. "Pray to God," the voice insisted. "But I don't know how to pray."

PRAYER CHANGES EVERYTHING

Suddenly Howard remembered how he had gone to church as a little boy and learned prayers there. "All I could recall were bits and pieces. As I began to mutter these things, trying my best to remember, the people around me became very, very agitated and angry and telling me that there was no God, that nobody could hear me, and that now they were going to make it much worse for me than what they'd already done.

"But I noticed that when I mentioned God, it drove them away. It was as if they couldn't stand being in the presence of that name. It finally drove them away completely and I was left alone to think about my life. An incalculable amount of time passed, as I considered everything I had done and said and thought. And I realized that my life was devoid of anything except my own selfish desires and that the people who had brought me to this place had been ruled by the same self-serving ends.

"My life, I now understood, was absent of love, absent of light, absent of hope, absent of all good things. It was, in short, utter darkness. I was just like them—ripping and tearing and biting and trying to dominate others. I was one of them. I had the veneer of being a nice guy, a respected college professor and all that, but in my heart was just my own neediness."

In that desperate moment, he remembered sitting in a Sunday school classroom as a child, singing "Jesus Loves Me." "Not only did I remember the words, but I remembered as a child believing in something other than myself."

Howard Storm called out to Jesus, "Please save me." He says, "I called out in the hope that He still might exist, and that He still might remember me, not really knowing if He would even care. It was my only hope."

Jesus was there. He remembered His child Howard Storm, and He did care.

Howard's eyes glistened with tears as he said, "And He came to me then, and reached down in the darkness, bathed in brilliant white light that allowed me to finally see myself as I was, nothing but a mass of blood and gore from what had been done to me. He reached down and touched me and all my wounds disappeared, and I was made whole. But more importantly, He filled me with a love that I can't possibly begin to describe. There are no words adequate to express His love for us and His love, specifically, for me in that moment.

"With that, He picked me up and put His arms around me and held me very tight against Him and stroked my back as I cried and wept for joy. I realized that not only did He love me—not in some kind of condescending way—but that He really *liked* me as a friend. It was, in fact, as if I'd found the best friend I'd ever known. He really knew me, more than my parents, more than my wife; He really *knew* me.

"Eventually, we left that place. We just went directly up and out, moving faster and faster, and off in the distance I saw that we were approaching a world of light, and I had a huge moment of trepidation, thinking that we were going to heaven and that this was not good because I felt that I was such filth, pure garbage, so unworthy.

"I said to myself, 'He has made a terrible mistake. I don't belong here.' And with that we stopped and He spoke to me for the first time and said, 'We don't make mistakes. You do belong here.'"

Howard recalls undergoing a complete review of his life. Then, "Jesus asked me if I had any questions, and I told Him I had a million of them. He told me to ask what I wanted, and I asked Him everything I could think of, and He answered everything patiently, kindly."

Howard recalls asking, "Why did You make me with such an inquiring mind? Why was I never satisfied with the easy answers?" Jesus replied, "Giving you that kind of mind was a great gift...but the problem was you were never satisfied with the answers once you got them."

Howard shook his head, "He told me that I was never willing to accept the truth, when the truth was right there. He knew me better than I knew myself."

I could see the wheels turning in Howard's mind as he thought about how to explain the next part.

"We also talked about what happens when people die," he said, "and some of His answers may seem simple, because the way Jesus explained things was really not that complicated. Anybody can get it. And I think I got it, and I hope I'm representing it exactly the way He told me. When people have a love of God and express that love in their life, they are attracted to God and He is attracted to them. It is literally like a magnet. The angels come and take those people to heaven where they become more perfect beings, enjoying eternity with God. People who don't like God and have rejected Him are repelled by Him. Although God doesn't want anybody to reject Him, and it is His desire that everyone find a home with

Him—God doesn't make people go to hell. People who reject God get exactly their desire. And they get to go to a place where they're not going to be bothered by God anymore. They take every good thing that God gives us in this world for granted. But in hell, all the good things that God gives us are totally absent, because we have rejected them all, including the gift of life. Consequently, there is no goodness there, there's no beauty there. It has all been rejected. It's like a bunch of rats in a cage."

THE FUN CENTER OF THE UNIVERSE

"When we finished talking, I told Jesus I wanted to go to heaven and be with Him forever. I know it sounds strange, but heaven is the fun center of the universe and I wanted more than anything to be part of it. But, instead, He told me that I was going to go back to this world to report what I had seen and experienced...I needed to come back and live a life that would make me suitable for heaven. Once I'd seen what I'd seen, all I wanted to do was stay there for eternity. I really believe that if people caught a glimpse of heaven, we would have a problem with them not wanting to stay here at all."

Eventually, Howard Storm found himself back in his hospital bed in Paris, experiencing the same horrendous pain in his stomach.

"In the next moment, a nurse came into the room. It was about 9 o'clock at night. And she told me that a doctor had finally arrived and that they were going to do the surgery immediately...it was, of course, successful, as it was meant to be all along."

When I asked Howard why he thought he was chosen to come back from death, he thought a moment, and then said, "I think there are several important reasons. When I was a child of twelve, I asked my pastor to baptize me and he did; second, I had a student who was a nun and I found out later she had been praying for me from the day she met me in 1974 and had all the other nuns praying for me, too. Last but most importantly, the Bible says in four different places that anyone who calls upon the name of the Lord will be saved. I had called out His name and He had answered me. People ask me all the time why they can't believe like I believe. I tell them that if they really want to know, ask Jesus sincerely, and He will show them the truth. He says if we ask for the good gifts—He's not going to give us junk like luxury cars and yachts—but He is going to give us what we want. And of course the greatest gift that we can ask for is faith. I asked Him and He gave it to me."

What was the most important thing he learned? "God is very disappointed with what we've done. He sent the prophets and the teachers to teach people how to be His children. And many of them turned their back and failed to learn. So God sent His only Son, Jesus, who would not only teach us but show us the way to heaven. He did the work so that we will all be guaranteed salvation if we only listen to Him and follow His example. And the world has even rejected that. It was supposed to be a life-changing event, a world-changing event. We don't have to live the way we are living, in fear and war and with people in want while others have more than they need. To love God and to love your neighbor as yourself is what Jesus came to teach us.

"Because of our fallen nature, it's hard for us to learn that lesson, but if we ask God, He will show us the way. Just say to Him, 'Give me compassion. Give me faith. Give me a purpose and some insight into why I'm here in the first place.' If you are asking for those things, and you really want them, He will give them to you."

Howard Storm's Near-Death Experience drastically changed his life. The former atheist university professor now serves God as pastor of Zion United Church of Christ in Cincinnati, Ohio.

Chapter 11

DR. GARY L. WOOD

IT'S EASY TO UNDERSTAND why Dr. Gary Wood is one of the most perennially popular speakers on the Christian lecture circuit. He is an outgoing and articulate man who impressed me with his sincerity. His riveting account of his 1966 Near-Death Experience is very much in line with the Bible's depiction of heaven. He told me that the Bible is not using metaphors when it describes heaven. He says the gates made of pearl really exist. So do the streets of gold. He experienced "The River of Life," with trees growing along the banks of the river that are for the healing of the nations.

In his book *A Place Called Heaven,* Gary explains that his parents were both alcoholics who were abusive to him and his little sister, Sue. "The Lord had His hand on our lives. While we were still so small and helpless, my parents decided that their lives would be simpler without the burden of raising Sue and I, so they left us on the porch steps of my maternal grandparents' house…. My grandparents showed us the kind of love that God has for us by adopting us as their own children."[1]

Gary learned about God from his grandparents and committed his life to the Lord when he was just six years of age. As a high school student in Farmington, New Mexico, he began to know for certain that God was calling him into the ministry. He loved to sing and for three years in a row was named "Outstanding Soloist" among high school students in the state of New Mexico. He planned to use his love of music, and his talent, as an integral part of his ministry.

After graduating from high school, he attended Wayland Baptist University in Plainview, Texas. He was a freshman there when he was involved in the horrible automobile accident that changed his life forever.

He was home for the Christmas holidays when he and his sister, Sue, borrowed their grandfather's car to visit some friends. They were on their way home, and only about a mile from their house, when the accident occurred.

He recalls that he and Sue were singing "Silent Night," when she suddenly screamed out in terror. Gary turned and saw that they were going to crash into the back of a truck. There was no time to stop—no time even to hit the brakes. There was an explosion, a momentary pain—and Gary was enveloped by a brilliant light.

His neck was broken in three places, his vocal cords were severed and his larynx was crushed. His head and face were sliced open with a gash that took 100 stitches to close. Gary's body was a mess. But his soul was soaring.

"The doctors at the scene pronounced me dead and turned to work on my sister," he told me. "She had gone through the windshield because, back in those days, they didn't have safety belts. They didn't even try to revive me. As far as they were concerned, I was already gone."

DYING WAS EASY

Gary says he had no fear.

"Dying was the most peaceful and tranquil experience I ever had in my life," he smiles. "The first thing that happened was that I came straight out of my body. I was caught up in a massive, swirling, funnel-shaped cloud and bright, brilliant light. I saw my body lying over the steering wheel, but by that time, I was already caught up in heaven. It was the most serene experience I've ever had in my life—joyful, exuberant, happy."

Dr. Wood told me that angels came to escort him to heaven, singing songs of praise as they did so. "You've never heard singing until you've heard an angel choir," he laughs.

Arriving in heaven, Gary saw the twelve gates of the Holy City. He was granted access and began walking down a broad boulevard. There he encountered John, his best friend from high school who had been killed in a car crash the previous year. The crash that killed John had been so violent that he had been decapitated, but in heaven he was perfectly whole.

"I learned from him that everyone who arrives in heaven is assigned someone to meet them and take them around. He looked exactly like I remembered him. He was young and handsome and there was no sign of his injuries. There were no wrinkles or deformities, and it's like I tell young people—there are no pimples in heaven."

When I asked him about other people in heaven, he told me that he'd seen children there, but everyone else seemed to be in their 30s, strong and healthy, with no imperfections.

"John and I embraced each other, and he took me to a library with volumes and volumes of scrolls containing prayer requests and the number of souls we have won to the Lord, and I saw the Lamb's Book of Life. He opened it up and I saw my name actually written in its pages. And it said, 'Paid in full by the precious red blood of Jesus.'"

When I asked him what else he had seen in heaven, Gary told of angels carrying bowls filled with the tears of people on earth that had been gathered up to be presented to God. He says he visited the throne room of God, where he saw a menorah and a shofar made of gold—which he believes is the instrument that will be played at the time of the Rapture (see 1 Thessalonians 4:16).

He described a beautiful river, "which in the Bible is called the River of Life (Revelation 22:1). Then my friend actually took me down into the river, and I saw people there clothed in sleeveless garments of linen and velvet—just as the high priests had worn in ancient Jewish ceremonies. I went down into the river and picked up golden nuggets bigger than my fist. And the light of the city—being Jesus—shone on the nuggets, producing an array of colors I can't begin to describe. It was just magnificent."

Several of the people I interviewed told me they will always remember the music they heard in heaven. Dr. Wood, who has always had a deep love of music, is no exception, although he said he was shocked to see a huge choir singing, "All Hail the Power of Jesus' Name." "It was the same song we have here on earth. And I turned to my friend and asked, 'Why are they singing Hymn Number 132 in the Baptist Hymnal?' And he told me that all songs in the spirit originate in heaven."

CLAPPING TREES AND SINGING FLOWERS

Gary also told me that trees clap in heaven. "This is the honest truth of what I saw—their branches and leaves actually applauding. The flowers had faces and they sang along with everything else. Everything in heaven gives worship and praise to the Lord God, in a real and literal sense. There was nothing symbolic or metaphorical about what I saw and experienced. It was as real as anything here on earth, only more so.

"I saw an area where there were little children gathered on the grass, rolling around playing with a lion like you would play with a fluffy kitten. I saw kinds of animals in heaven that I've never seen before. People ask me if they'll be reunited with their pets in heaven, and I tell them that if it's part of God's plan, then they surely will."

Then the most thrilling moment of Gary's time in heaven: "I met Jesus face to face, and He was the most wonderful, amazing person. When I saw Him I fell at His feet and He reached down and picked me up. He stands a little taller than the average Jewish man, about 6 feet 2 inches…He is most definitely Jewish, and was wearing a prayer shawl with fringes. I also saw the scars on His hands, His feet, and on His head. And He had blue eyes. Jewish people from the tribe of Judah are known to have blue eyes."

Like the others I talked to, Gary told me he wanted to stay in heaven and be with Jesus forever. But it was not to be.

"John said to me, 'You've got to go back. She's using that name.'"

Gary's little sister was crying out to Jesus to bring her brother back from the dead. Some sixty minutes after he had been declared dead, life returned to Gary's body. "I discovered later that I had been commissioned to make heaven real to this generation. That's why I was returned to earth."

Gary says that after returning to his body, he went through nine difficult months of recovery. "It wasn't easy. Because of my accident and all the reconstructive surgery I underwent, I was in excruciating pain." Because his vocal cords had been severed in the accident, he couldn't talk. He loved to sing and had a voice that touched many hearts for God, but he knew those days were behind him.

"Then one day I heard a song on the radio. It was 'He Touched Me,' and while that song was being played, Jesus walked into my hospital room, put His hand on my throat, and I was suddenly able to speak. A nurse came into the room and said, 'Good morning,' and I answered her saying, 'Praise God, I've been healed!' And she dropped her tray right then and there."

Today, Gary's voice is stronger than ever, and he loves to sing God's praises.

"The truth is, my vocal cords are still severed. Medical doctors have examined me and confirmed this. A lot of skeptics come to my meetings trying to disprove my story, and after they see me and the X-rays that were taken, they end up accepting Jesus. It's a notable miracle every time I open my mouth.

"I came back with a message," he says, "Jesus told me to tell people never to buy in to the condemnation of the devil that they're unworthy. 'Tell them they are worthy because I redeemed them with My blood.' He said that there will be a spirit of restoration that will occur prior to His return. He also said there will be a strong emphasis on prayer and a great outburst of miracles. We're on the verge of the greatest miracle revival the world has ever seen to usher in the return of the Messiah."

Chapter 12

DON PIPER

An ordained minister since 1985, Don Piper came to international recognition with the publication of his *New York Times* best-selling book, *90 Minutes in Heaven*. Don's story differs from other Near-Death Experiences in that he was declared both clinically and biologically dead after a terrible car accident instantly snuffed out his life. As he says, he didn't have a Near-Death Experience, he had a "Total Death Experience." His description of heaven remains one of the most compelling and convincing on record.

When I asked Don to tell me what happened to him, he replied, "I was killed instantly in a terrible car crash. When you're dead an hour and a half, you're not nearly dead—you're totally dead. Four paramedics pronounced me dead at the scene of the accident. I'm only here because people prayed and God said, 'Yes.'"

Don's accident happened on the morning of January 18, 1989, when he was on his way home from a pastor's conference. It was a cold, windy, and rainy day. Gary was traveling at around 50 miles per hour as the road was unfamiliar to him and visibility was low. "It was right around noon and I was crossing a rural bridge in East Texas. An 18-wheeler, going about 60 miles an hour, veered across the center stripe and hit me head-on. It literally rolled over the top of my car, instantly crushing me. It was a horrific crash, and he struck a couple of more cars after he hit me. It was a very isolated area and took a long time for help to arrive."

When paramedics finally reached the scene they were astounded to find that Don was the only one hurt.

"All of them were working on me, trying to bring me back and resuscitate me, trying to restore my life. But I was absent from the body and present with the Lord. That's my best evidence that all this really happened. The moment I took the last breath on that bridge, I was standing at the gates of heaven."

Back in Texas, Don's body was so badly mangled that paramedics put a tarp over his car. The windows were broken out and they didn't want anyone else to see what had happened to him because it was so gruesome. They waited for the medical examiner to come and sign the death certificate so they could remove the body.

"As I would learn later, the major bones were now missing, so my lower left arm was just a piece of flesh that held the hand to the rest of the arm. It was the same with the left leg... Four and a half inches of femur were missing and never found. The doctors have no medical explanation why I didn't lose all the blood in my body."

Paramedics estimated Don's time of death as 11:45 a.m. At 1:15 p.m., 90 minutes later, they checked again to make sure he was dead. He was.

"During the whole time I was gone, it was just a shell of me that was left in the car. I didn't have the experience of looking down at myself from above or going through a tunnel. I was just instantly bathed in a brilliant light, so bright that you would be blinded by it with earthly eyes, but I no longer had earthly eyes. I was in heaven. It was instantaneous. One second I was taking my last breath on the bridge, and the next I was standing outside one of the twelve gates of heaven."

Don says he knew where he was from the second he arrived. He found himself standing in front of a group of people he had known and loved all his life.

A Reunion in Heaven

"And they all looked good, really good. If you want to look good, heaven is where you want to be. I was actually having a homecoming, a reunion with my loved ones, and when I saw their faces I knew where I was because I knew where they were."

He says his friends and loved ones seemed to know he was coming. "They were waiting for me, like a welcoming committee. But you have a reservation to get in. The Bible says that any time anyone makes a decision to go to heaven through Christ [Messiah], there is a big celebration up there, and your name is written in the Lamb's Book of Life."

Among the members of Don's "welcoming committee" was his beloved grandfather, who had died suddenly of a heart attack. "We were very close. I often say that I've got a lot of broken bones, but nothing hurts worse than a broken heart. And when my grandfather died, it broke my heart."

Don told me that his grandfather had lost some fingers as the result of industrial accidents, "but when he held out his hands to me, nothing was missing."

Others who were on hand to meet Don included aunts and uncles, teachers, a couple of classmates, his former next door neighbor, and some people he hadn't seen in years and had almost forgotten. Everyone had played some important role in the development of Don's faith.

"They took me to church, they modeled Christian life, and they told me about Jesus so that I would know how to go to heaven. And they greeted me at the gates when I got there. Which of course brings up the question for all of us: Who are we going to greet? Who's going to be there because of us? I think that's part of the reason we're still here.

"They were all perfect in every way. There were no scars on them or blemishes of any sort. And I knew every one of them by name. For instance, Mrs. Norris, my next door neighbor, was standing next to me. And she was the one who used to take me to church with her on Sunday because my dad was gone a lot and my mother didn't know how to drive.

"I can remember her car pulling up and her saying, 'Honey, would you like to go to the Lord's House?' And I'd say, 'Yes ma'am, I surely would.' And I would climb into the car, and I knew somebody cared about me."

The reunion with his loved ones was thrilling and joyous. Even so, that isn't what Don remembers most about his time in heaven. "My most vivid memory, and I wouldn't have thought this to be the case, was the music that surrounded me and invaded me. There were so many songs that were glorifying God, thousands of them really, that were rendered at the same time without chaos because they all fit and interfaced with each other. And soaring above all those songs was 'Holy, Holy, Holy,' because that's what He is. I can close my eyes and still hear it as if I was there right now. The only thing that comes close to it in terms of its magnitude is the 'Hallelujah Chorus.' But there are other songs that are not quite that regal, even some of our praise songs, that come close. It happens in a wide variety of music, because God inhabits the praises of His people."

Don believes that worshiping God is one of the primary things we will do when we get to heaven. "It's unlike any other worship we've ever experienced. And that's really saying something, because we've all had powerful worship experiences down here. But they really can't compare. There in heaven, it's a way of life—dining at the Lord's Table and praising God."

When I asked Don if he saw Jesus in heaven, he replied that he did—but only from a distance. "I was going to Him, and I was very excited. I just wanted to go through the gate, up the street, and fall at His feet and say thank You. But it wasn't to be. God had other plans for me. My time in heaven was almost up.

"Of course in heaven there is no time, so I was unsure if I was there ninety minutes or ninety years. It's hard for us to wrap our brains around it, but everything exists in an eternal state. And when you're there, you are eternal as well. I know that I was absent from the earth for ninety minutes."

Before he could get to Jesus, Don was suddenly back in his demolished car—and there was someone standing beside him.

"It was a pastor who came to the crash site, and God told him, 'You've got to pray for the man in the red car.' That was me. So he got permission to crawl into the wreckage and pray over my dead body, singing the great old hymn, "What a Friend We Have in Jesus." He's singing that song, holding on to my body under the tarp—and suddenly I start singing it with him. He got out of the car really fast and told the police, 'The dead man is singing.'"

HEAVEN IS REAL

As Don says, "That was the beginning of the rest of my life here on earth. I was pulled back into my body from heaven. People prayed and God said, 'Yes.' I am an answered prayer. I was sent back with a message. The message is simple: heaven is real. It's a real place and God wants you to go there. But you're going to have to trust Jesus. He said, 'I am the way, the truth, and the life. No one comes to the Father except through me.' Heaven is real and Jesus is the way. It's as simple as that.

"Heaven is a biblical heaven, which means there is also a biblical hell. Where you go depends on the decisions you make here on earth. But you're going to go somewhere. This life is not the end. It's only the beginning. Just because you live a good life and have some kind of spiritual awareness isn't going to get you into heaven. It's all about the relationship you have with Jesus."

Chapter 13

BILL WIESE

BILL WIESE WENT TO hell at 3 a.m. on November 23, 1998.

Twenty-three minutes later, his wife, Annette, was awakened by his screams.

She found him on the living room floor, trembling in fear. "Pray for me! Pray for me!" he screamed. "The Lord has taken me to hell." It took her a while to get her husband calmed down. When she finally managed to do it, he asked her for a glass of water.

Bill is quick to explain that his time in hell was not a Near-Death Experience or an out-of-body experience. It was, rather, a vision. But that doesn't mean it was a dream. Bill believes he was in a spiritual body and that everything he experienced in those 23 minutes was just as real as if he had been cast into hell in the flesh. He felt pain. He suffered from thirst. He struggled for breath. And he dealt with real, palpable fear.

"Look at Second Corinthians 12:2," he says. "In that Scripture, Paul says, 'I know a man in Christ [Messiah] who fourteen years ago was caught up to the third heaven. Whether it was in the body or out of the body I do not know—God knows.' A vision can be so real that you don't know whether it's a real vision or a real, physical experience" (NIV).

Bill also points to Ezekiel, where the prophet says, "...while I was sitting in my house and the elders of Judah were sitting before me, the hand of the Sovereign Lord came on me there. ...He stretched out what looked like a hand and took me by the hair of my head. The Spirit lifted me up between earth and heaven and in visions of God he took me to Jerusalem, to the entrance of the north gate of the inner court, where the idol that provokes to jealousy stood" (Ezekiel 8:1-3 NIV). It was a vision, and yet Ezekiel felt himself taken to Jerusalem.

Bill Wiese says he had never had a vision before. He was a normal guy, a real estate broker who went to work every day, and a Christian for over 25 years. He describes himself as having a conservative nature, and not the sort of person who likes to be in the spotlight. He had no advance warning that God was about to give him a vision of hell. When I asked why God chose him for such an experience, he simply said he doesn't know. "I'm not a Billy Graham," he says. "I'm just an ordinary guy. Besides, summer weather is too hot for me."

What he does know is that he suddenly found himself falling through a tunnel and landing face down on a hard, stone floor.

"The first thing I noticed was the heat," he says. "It was unbearably hot. I wondered how I could even be alive. I should have been incinerated."

GASPING FOR BREATH

In the next moment, he was overwhelmed by a nauseating odor. "It was like an open sewer, only one thousand times worse," Bill remembers. "The air was full of burning sulfur. I had to gasp and fight for even the tiniest bit of air."

When Bill looked around, he saw that he was in a dark, dank cell. The walls and floor were made of stone. Rusted iron bars closed off any possibility of escape. As he described the cell in which he found himself, I thought of a dungeon from medieval times. Bill said his mind turned to Isaiah 24:22 (NIV): "They will be herded together like prisoners bound in a dungeon; they will be shut up in prison and be punished after many days." He also reminded me that Proverbs 7:27 speaks of "chambers of death."

He tried to get up, but found it took tremendous effort to move. He remembered all the verses that talk about God being our strength. God was not present in hell, and so there was no strength for those who were condemned to go there—but only weakness and fatigue.

Tragically for Bill Wiese, his ordeal was just beginning. He was suddenly aware there were two creatures in the cell with him. They seemed to be a mixture of human and reptile, with scales covering their bodies and long, vicious-looking claws. They stamped around the cell, cursing and blaspheming God. Hate for everyone and everything shone from their eyes—and they were about to take it out on Bill.

"One of them picked me up like I was nothing but a glass of water, and threw me against the wall. It hurt terribly, and yet I knew, somehow, that God was protecting me from feeling the full extent of it. Then the other creature picked me up, stuck his claws into my chest and began tearing me open. I couldn't believe I wasn't dead."

Bill says he was surprised that no blood came out of his terrible wounds. "But then I remembered that the Bible says the life is in the blood (Leviticus 17:11), and there is no life in hell."

Bill went on, "At that moment, something grabbed me out of the cell and placed me by this pit of fire, about a mile across. Heat from the flames was intense. Brimstone, like lava, was falling into the pit from above. I could see the outlines of people burning in the fire, and I was listening to the screams. Millions of people were screaming in agony—and the noise was deafening. If you've ever heard someone screaming in terror, you know what a terrible sound that can be. Multiply that by ten thousand and you'll begin to have some idea of what it's like in hell."

He shook his head at the horror of the memory. "This wasn't an allegorical or a metaphorical fire. It was real, literal fire. There are forty-six verses in the New Testament that mention about hell. Eighteen of those talk about fire."

What else did Bill Wiese find in hell?

- Maggots: The ground and walls were covered with them.

- Darkness: So deep and heavy you could feel it.

- Isolation: People in hell were kept apart from one another. There was no conversation or friendship.

- Fear: "I was constantly afraid, and it was worse than any fear I'd ever felt before." Bill told me that when he was a teenager, he had been with a group of surfers who were attacked by tiger sharks off the coast of Florida. One young man lost a leg in the attack. A shark took a bite out of Bill's surfboard. "I was afraid that day," he said. "But the fear in hell was much, much worse."

- Thirst: In hell, Bill said, he felt like he'd been running through the Sahara Desert with cotton in his mouth.

- Hopelessness: "Somehow, when I was in hell, God hid it from me that I was saved. I think He did this because He wanted me to understand the utter horror of knowing that you can never get out of hell. I thought about my wife, and how I would never see her again. She had no idea I had come to this terrible place. In this life, we always have hope. But in hell, there is no hope."

Bill told me that he is sometimes asked if the existence of a hell like the one he describes doesn't make it seem that God is cruel. He shook his head.

"What they don't understand is that hell is the way it is because God withdrew His attributes from hell—so what you have left is a place without God. Hell is dark because God is light. There's only death in hell because God is life. There's only hatred in hell because God is love. There's no mercy there because God is merciful. When God removes Himself from a place, all the good goes with Him."

Hope returned to Bill Wiese when he was pulled out of hell and into the presence of a Person who shone with bright light. "The light was so bright I could only see His outline, but I knew immediately who it was. I fell down at His feet and said, 'Jesus!'

He replied, 'I am.' I knew then that because He went to the cross, I didn't have to go to that horrible place. All I could do was worship Him and say over and over, 'Thank You, Jesus.'"

It wasn't until three months later, at a Bible study, that Bill finally shared the story of what had happened to him. "I'm a conservative person. I wasn't comfortable talking about this, but then God said to me, 'It's not about you being comfortable, it's about you being obedient.'"

Over the next several years, Bill and Annette Wiese spent much of their time traveling the country and sharing Bill's account of his trip to hell. "We paid our own way," Bill says. "We didn't take a dime."

He also says he wrote his book because a publisher heard his story and approached him, and not the other way around. He feels that God wants him to share his story, not to bring people under condemnation, but to warn them.

"When I met Jesus, He wept because He didn't want people to go to hell. It's way past our knowledge to understand how much He loves us. All we have to do is be humble enough to admit we're sinners, accept what Jesus has done in our behalf, and He'll save us."

Chapter 14

CURTIS "EARTHQUAKE" KELLEY

AT 58 YEARS OF age, Bishop Curtis "Earthquake" Kelley still has the solid build of an athlete. It's easy to believe that he was once a promising heavyweight boxer. He was managed by the legendary Don King, until an automobile accident ended his career. He looks like he could still handle himself in the ring, but he's such a friendly, likeable man that it's difficult to imagine him doing anything the least bit violent. By his own admission, Kelley was once a gangster, dealing drugs and running with a violent crowd. Today, he's pastor of The Bridge of Deliverance International Church in Hollywood, California. The love of God shines in his eyes. He left the gangster lifestyle many years ago.

He is the only person I interviewed who says he has been to both heaven and hell. His experience in hell came after a drug overdose when he was fifteen. Some 36 years later, he spent a brief period in heaven after suffering a brain aneurism.

Earthquake was one of ten children born into a family with an unpredictable and violent father. The man pretended to be a Christian but was, in reality, heavily into voodoo. As a result, Kelley—who was called Kirk by his family—was introduced to the occult at a very young age. His mother, on the other hand, was a dedicated Christian who constantly prayed for her children. It was her prayers, in fact, that brought Kelley back from hell, even though he told me that he knew he belonged there and deserved the "torment and great pain" he experienced.

Earthquake told me he was five years old when his father brought a priestess into the home to teach him all about voodoo. For the next several years, he says, "I got about two hours of sleep every night, because I had to spend so much time learning about voodoo." He learned how to cast various types of spells and curses, memorized the names of the various spirits connected to the religion, and often saw spirits in his room at night. If he didn't spend enough time at his "studies," his father beat him. He was beaten for many other offenses too, and sometimes just because his father had drunk too much or was in a bad mood.

"I grew up in the projects of Stamford, Connecticut, where my older brothers had what we called a street corner pharmacy business," Earthquake said. "From the time I was four years old, I was around people shooting up heroin. I saw people murdered. I saw women gang-raped. I didn't know what it was like to be a child."

ON THE ROAD TO HELL

Earthquake was fascinated by what heroin did to people. To him, it seemed that getting high was like going into another world—and he wanted to try it. It seemed like a good way to escape the pressures of daily life with his unpredictable and violent father.

"My brothers told me I was too young to use heroin," he said. "That's when a voice spoke to me and said, 'I'll tell you how to get high.'" The spirit told him how to get high by burning his plastic toys and sniffing the fumes. After that, he got high every day.

At the age of five, he began running numbers for his father. He started smoking marijuana at the age of six, and quickly moved on to cocaine, heroin, and other drugs.

All this time, Earthquake's mother was steadfast in prayer for him and his siblings. She often proclaimed over them, "My children will be saved and great shall be the salvation of my children." At the time, it seemed like nothing more than wishful thinking. Her children were on the fast track away from God, and it would take a miracle to bring them back.

In 1971, the family moved to Milwaukee at their mother's urging. She believed God had spoken to her and told her the family should move to Wisconsin. Perhaps she felt that moving her family halfway across the country would turn things around for her children and get them off drugs. If so, it didn't work. At least, not at first.

Earthquake and his brothers immediately got involved in the drug trade in Milwaukee and began making big money selling cocaine. "At the age of fifteen, I was making at least $200 a day. We were making so much money we threw away the one dollar bills." By his own count he had seen 54 of his acquaintances die. "People had pulled guns on me more times than I could count. I had been attacked by rival gang members."

Earthquake didn't realize it, but he was on the road to hell. Literally.

In his book *Bound to Lose, Destined to Win,* he describes what happened:

> One hot summer day in 1971, my brother Bobby and his friend Bill decided to go to a bar along the waterfront. "Can I go, too?" I asked. "No. You're too young."
>
> They planned to leave within an hour and head to the bar. In the meantime I heard a voice—that same voice I heard in Stamford, Connecticut, at the age of four. This time it was a very enthusiastic voice that said, "All these years you've been getting high. But it doesn't last long. You need to get super-high. You've never been really high. Why don't you try getting super-high?"[1]

That's what he did. He mixed potent pills that, by themselves, could have kept him high for days. He added cocaine, marijuana, and beer—after talking his brother and his friend into letting him go with them to the bar.

"By the time we arrived in Lake Michigan, I was so high that I was staggering when I got out of the car. Bobby and Bill laughed because they thought it was hilarious. I was proud to show them what a man I was."

For a while, Earthquake sat in the bar, enjoying the feeling of being high. The afternoon sun was shining through the window and the warmth felt good.

Then, suddenly, everything went dark.

"It was pitch black," he remembers. "Then I saw spirits, perhaps fifty of them, come out of the floor."

They grabbed at him and hit him. It seemed they were trying to pull him back down through the floor they had come up through. Fearing that he was overdosing, Earthquake begged his brother to take him home, but Bobby just laughed.

"Take me home to Mom," Earthquake pleaded. He wanted his mother to pray for him, because he knew that if she did, he would be all right.

"They made fun of me...but I kept pleading with them until they reluctantly agreed to take me home. They helped me into the back of the car, and they sat in front, complaining the whole time about having to take me home."

The demons had momentarily let go of Earthquake while his companions helped him out to the car—but they weren't finished with him yet.

INTO THE ABYSS

"All of a sudden the demons came up through the floor of the car. They grabbed me by my mouth, pulled my spirit out of my body, and dragged me down through the bottom of the car." He still remembers vividly how he saw the drive shaft underneath the car, and the wheels spinning around. "I had never been underneath a car before, but I saw exactly what it's like. There's no way I could have imagined that."

The demon spirits dragged Earthquake down into the earth. "I saw sewer pipes, rocks, and everything else that was inside the earth." He was carried to a place that he describes as being "red and black," and dumped roughly onto a hard floor.

"I can't even begin to tell you what they were doing to me. Pain was hitting me from all sides. The torment was nonstop. But I knew I was where I deserved to be."

At one point, Earthquake says he tried to make a run for it. But the demons quickly surrounded him and began beating him again. "They continued to laugh at me, mock me, and remind me of every bad thing I had ever done. They tormented me in ways that I don't want to talk about."

He says that just when all hope was gone, a huge pair of hands that seemed to be made of pure light reached down into hell and gently lifted him up above the mob that was trying to tear him apart.

"They were screaming, 'He's ours! He belongs to us!' But their cries went unheeded."

Earthquake, still cradled in those hands, went back up through the earth. Up past the rocks, the sewer pipes, up past everything he had seen on the way down—and then out of the earth, through the undercarriage of the car, and back into his body, which was still sprawled in the back seat.

That's when he heard a voice say, "Because of your mother's prayers, and because you were chosen by God, you have been spared."

Of course, Earthquake was relieved and exhilarated to be out of hell, but his torment was not over. The drugs he took had caused serious damage to his body. He was partially blind, paralyzed from the waist down, and could not tend to his own basic needs. I won't go into the rest of the story, except to say that by God's grace he recovered completely, surrendered his life to the Lord, and eventually became a well-known and respected pastor.

Flash forward 34 years to 2004. Earthquake was at a meeting with other pastors when he suddenly felt as if hot water was being poured into his head. "Every time I turned my head, it seemed like I felt an electrical shock." The symptoms persisted for two days, before his wife convinced him to go to the hospital.

The diagnosis was quick and frightening—a brain aneurysm.

Bishop Kelley was rushed to the intensive care unit where doctors began treatments they hoped would save his life.

One night, alone in the hospital, the "end" came. "Suddenly I felt as though I had separated from my body. I was light as a feather as I hovered over my body and looked at the guy who was lying in the bed with tubes in his arm and an oxygen cord up his nose. I thought to myself, 'This guy is in terrible shape. It doesn't look like he's going to make it.'

"Then it occurred to me that the person I was looking at was me. I had no idea I was that bad off. I thought, 'Earthquke Kelley, you're gone. When the nurses come in, they're going to find you dead.' I didn't feel any sorrow, but I wondered what was going to happen next. Would I just hang around the ceiling? And how could I be at the ceiling looking down at my body that appeared to be dead?"

THE RIVER OF LIFE

The next thing he knew, he found himself standing next to a tall, muscular angel with enormous wings that seemed to emit sparks of gold whenever he moved. "I'm six foot five, but this angel must have been at least seven and a half feet tall," Earthquake says.

He was no longer in the hospital, but standing on grassy, green fields beside a beautiful sparkling river. Kelley recalls that the angel said, "Walk around," so that's what he did.

He walked along the banks of the river, the water of which seemed to be made of thousands of sparkling diamonds. "I kept thinking of that song, 'I Have a River of Life Flowing Out of Me.'" He strolled across the green grass and noticed that each blade seemed to be inlaid with diamonds and emeralds.

"I was so excited, I didn't think about being dead. I had been in pain—now the pain was gone."

Just across the river was a magnificent city with buildings that seemed to be made of pure gold. The gold seemed purer, brighter, than anything he had seen before—as if the substance we called "gold" is just a pale imitation of the real thing.

People were gathering on the opposite side of the river bank. "I saw some of the saints of God that I had been to their home-going service." Earthquake remembers that they were smiling and happy to see him. But they did not beckon him to join them.

"I asked them, 'Can I come over?' but they said, 'No, not now.' I could hear a choir of angels singing, and it was music that not only went in my ears, it touched me deep down inside."

Earthquake says that he kept walking along the river, looking across to the dazzlingly beautiful city and longing to join the happy souls who lived there. Suddenly he caught sight of someone on the other side of the river who made his heart swell with emotion.

Standing there with a huge smile on his face was his son, Scott, who had been murdered six years earlier at the age of twenty-four.

Earthquake's mind went back to the last time he had seen Scott, the day before he was murdered. The two of them had been in the kitchen pretending to box each other, and Earthquake recalls that his wife called out to them, "What are you boys doing in there?" And then to her husband, "Don't you hit my baby."

Earthquake teasingly replied that he was trying to toughen him up.

The truth was that Scott was an outstanding young man. A devoted son. A caring brother. A committed Christian with a heart for caring for the less fortunate.

Suddenly he stopped boxing, and a serious look came across his face. He grabbed his dad, hugged him close and said, "I love you, Dad. I'm so proud of you and Mom. Promise me that if anything happens, you and Mom will not stop helping people."

Earthquake was taken aback by his son's words. Did he feel that something was going to happen? And why was he worried that whatever it was, it might cause them to stop helping people?

The Kelleys lived in Watts, an area of Los Angeles that has much more than its share of gangs, violence, and poverty. They ran a center there where they provided food, shelter, and other help for the poor and needy. "We housed people from all walks of life— gang members from the Crips and the Bloods, drug addicts, the daughter of a man heavily involved in the pornography industry, politicians, sports figures, actors, and other people who worked in the film industry." In addition, "Our children—Scott, Zina, Angelia, Keme, Christopher, Cherish, and Curtis Junior—never knew what it was like to live in a house without other people in our home whom we ministered to and helped get back on their feet. It didn't matter to the people we helped that we lived in Watts. They came to our house anyway, and we protected them."

The day after the "boxing match" in the Kelley's kitchen— December 7, 1998—Earthquake was supposed to speak at a minister's convention in Las Vegas. He felt uneasy about going and thought about canceling. But the event had been scheduled for months in advance, and he hated to cancel at the last minute—so he went on as planned.

That's when he received devastating news.

Scott had been shot to death in an attempted carjacking. The shooter was a member of a family the Kelleys had helped numerous times. "The attacker knew exactly who he was shooting." Scott's brother, Curtis Jr., who was with him when the attack occurred, reported that Scott's last words were, "Hey man, I'm the Bishop's son." The assailant shot him anyway.

Only then did Earthquake understand what his son had meant when he asked his dad to promise that he would go on helping people no matter what happened.

And now, six years later, they stood smiling at each other across the River of Life. Earthquake remembers that his son looked handsome, strong, and full of life.

The moment Earthquake saw him, he called out, "Scott, it's you! You're alive!"

"Yes, Dad, I'm alive."

"Son, this place is really something."

"Dad, you and Mom told us for years about this place. It's so much better than anything you described."

Earthquake wanted desperately to give his son a hug.

"How can I cross over there? Is there a boat or something?"

Scott laughed and shook his head. "There's no boat coming for you, Dad. You can't cross this river because you must go back and finish the work God has for you to do. You must go back. Remember when you made me that promise? You're still helping the poor aren't you? Remember, Dad, you gave me your word."

Earthquake says he desperately wanted to stay in this paradise, but he knew he couldn't. He was given a glimpse of the world to come, and that would have to do for now. "Today, I am still walking around with a subarachnal aneurysm that the doctors say could kill me at any time. But I will not die until my mission on earth is finished. The enemy wants me dead, but it is God who holds my life in His hands. Only He will decide when it is time for me to go home to be with Him."

Earthquake says he didn't see Jesus, but he heard His voice. "I am sending you back to tell people to repent of all their sins. Tell them to pray from the depths of their heart. Tell them to fast and seek My face. Unless they repent, they will never see My Holy City."

Earthquake concludes, "Please hear me. Every moment of every day, people are dying lost and going to hell. What is more positive than wanting to keep people out of hell? I've been to hell. And I don't want anybody else to go there.

"I have been tormented, and I have heard the cries of those who are tormented and lost forever. If you spend eternity in hell, you constantly will be reminded of what a fool you were for listening to the devil's lies. You will replay every sermon you ever heard. You will remember every person who gave you an invitation to turn your life to Jesus. And you will spend eternity begging for another chance."

Chapter 15

DEAN BRAXTON

DEAN BRAXTON IS AN ordained Baptist minister. He and his wife, Marilyn, currently serve as assistant pastors at His Word Christian Center in Tacoma, Washington. They have been married 30 years and have six children. In May 2006, Dean had a Near-Death Experience that was remarkable for the vivid and lucid quality of what he saw and heard. Dean's testimony of his journey to heaven and his face-to-face meeting with Yeshua gives an unprecedented glimpse into just how glorious heaven really is. He also heard a message from Yeshua Himself that may startle you. I am sure that many church leaders would be startled to hear it.

Dean was clinically dead for one hour and 45 minutes, but says he was brought back to life by the persistent prayers of his wife and Christian friends. His journey to paradise began when he went into the hospital for a routine operation.

"I had kidney stones," he told me. "The doctor gave me an antibiotic to kill the infection. But it so happened he used the wrong medicine, so when they went to remove the stones they literally pushed the infection straight into my bloodstream."

The doctor's error caused Dean to go into septic shock. Poison spread throughout his body, causing his vital organs to shut down.

"Even though I was unconscious, I felt myself suffocating. I had almost drowned when I was a little kid and I knew the one way I didn't want to die was by suffocation. I knew what it was like, and I had asked the Lord not to let me go that way.

"But the odd thing was, I wasn't overwhelmed with shock or fear. I experienced no panic. Instead, I heard myself saying, 'I am going home.' And a peace and joy unlike anything I had ever known overcame me. I was not fearful because I knew where I was going."

Dean says he learned in those moments that your spirit doesn't leave after your body dies. "The spirit leaves the body and then you die," he told me. "I came to understand that, unlike what a lot of people think, that it's not your body kicking you out, but in reality it's you, kicking your body off. I found support for this in Scripture. What I like to tell people is that my experience didn't prove the Word of God, the Word of God proved my experience. And the Bible says, in the second chapter of James, that faith without works is dead, just like the body is dead without the spirit. So, when you die, it's your spirit leaving and then your body dying, not the other way around."

Dean's wife, Marilyn, had been at the hospital with her husband, but after finding out that his hospitalization might be longer than expected, she went home to get a change of clothes. "On her way home in the car, she got a call telling her that my heart had just stopped and that they were doing CPR on me."

As soon as she hung up, Marilyn starting calling people she knew would pray for her husband's recovery. By the time she was able to get back to the hospital, there were nine other people in the waiting room who had dropped everything and came directly to the hospital to pray for Dean.

MOVING TOWARD THE LIGHT

"In the end, the doctors worked on me for an hour and forty-five minutes, trying to bring me back to life. During that time, I was clinically dead and my spirit had already left my body. When that happened, again I understood in a new way the Scripture that says to be absent from the body is to be present with the Lord [see 2 Corinthians 5:8]. Faster than a person can blink, I was with Him. When I left my body I also left the hospital, the earth, and even this universe. I entered a very dark place with no light at all and what I saw in the distance was heaven getting closer."

Excitement shone in Dean's eyes as he described moving rapidly through the darkness toward a brilliant light, "brighter than you can ever imagine. I came to realize then that we really are children of the light. There was no darkness or shadow in that brilliance at all.

"Later, when this was all over, my wife was driving me home on a beautiful May afternoon. If you've ever been to the Northwest, you know that we don't get a lot of sunny days. But this one was beautiful, and I could see Mount Rainier clearly in the distance. I must have had a strange look on my face, so Marilyn asked me what was wrong, and I told her, 'It is so dull here.'

"Nothing compared to the light I saw coming from heaven as I moved closer toward it. Many people who have had the same kind of experience described it as like being in a tunnel. But it's really just moving toward the light that creates that impression, like a light at the end of the tunnel. In reality you are just moving through a great dark space toward a brilliant light."

Dean's amazement continued when he arrived in heaven.

"Everything was alive there," he says. "Since then I've gone back and searched the Scriptures. I found passages such as chapter 10 of Revelation when John talks about how the seven thunders spoke. In heaven, even the atmosphere is alive. He didn't say it 'sounded' like thunder. He says the seven thunders spoke. Chapter 8 speaks about an eagle flying around proclaiming words of knowledge, so you know that the animals there can speak. In chapter 16, it says, amazingly, that the altar spoke. That would be like a table or a chair speaking here on earth. God is a God of life. So everything He produces is alive. In chapter 19 of Revelation it says that even His throne is alive. So everything is alive when you enter in, and you are welcomed by everything. You know you're in the right place because everything there wants you there."

Dean says that heaven was clear and clean—the very air was a joy to breathe.

"We have gotten so accustomed to death and decay here that we filter it out. Every place has a smell, and if you live there long enough you get used to it. But in heaven, nothing is dying and the smell of decay is gone."

He also reported that heavenly colors are brighter and more vivid than those on earth, something I heard from almost everyone I interviewed who had visited heaven during a Near-Death

Experience. Dean says everything in heaven was wonderful, but the best experience of all was meeting Jesus face to face.

"When I saw Him for the first time all I could say was, 'You did this for me?' I knew the only reason I was there was because of what He did for me, and for us all, on the cross. All I could do was repeat over and over, 'Thank You, thank You, thank You!' Everything about me was praising Him. The first thing I praised Him for was when I saw how He was looking at me—as if I had never sinned in my life—like I never did anything wrong. Of course we know that when He forgives, He forgets. But it's one thing to have that knowledge and another to actually experience it personally. I was past just believing it: I was experiencing it, living it in the eternal moment."

When I asked if Jesus spoke to him, a smile spread across Dean's face.

"He spoke to me about a lot of things, but He specifically focused on the parable of the Prodigal Son. He said that the Prodigal Son was really the Jewish people.

"The Prodigal Son is the one the Father is calling back home. And the Jewish people are on their way home. He's looking for them, just like the father in the parable looked for the arrival of his long-lost son. Up to this point I had not interpreted the parable in this way. I always thought it was about a Christian who had gone astray and was coming back to the Lord. But what Jesus was emphasizing to me, more than anything else, was that as the Jewish people were returning to Him, the Christian church was not receiving them in the way He wanted. They were literally getting jealous, as the older son in the parable was jealous, telling his father how long he had been with him and served him.... And I love what the father said, which is, 'Everything I have is yours. But this is your brother. He was once lost but now is found. He was once dead but now he's alive.'

"I believe Jesus showed me this because it is what He wants to emphasize at this time in history. We are coming to the end of the age and He is calling the Jewish people back to Him."

Dean was just getting warmed up.

"There is what I call a culture in heaven. It is an eternal culture. It is the culture that God has asked us to live on this planet. It's about love and compassion and it's not a temporal thing. It's forever. For the same reason, all of our relationships here on earth will continue after we die. We will pick up where we left off with our loved ones in heaven. I have come to believe that the culture God gave the Jewish people was not simply meant for them. It was, instead, a heavenly culture. It's an eternal culture. It is more life-giving than we can imagine.

"One of those life-giving elements is the family. Family is so important in Jewish culture. When I arrived in heaven, all the members of my family who had come before me were there to greet me. Even though there were countless generations, I knew who each one was. The reason is the same as when Jesus was on the Mount of Transfiguration and Moses and Elijah were with him. Although the apostles had never seen them before, they knew who they were. It's that kind of special knowledge that you receive in heaven. When my relatives greeted me, I recognized some of them, but others had lived and died long before me. Yet we needed no introduction. It was generation after generation of those in my family who had accepted Jesus (Messiah) as Lord and Savior who were there to greet me. In heaven we have the opportunity to be that family we always wanted to be."

Like the others I talked to, Dean Braxton longs to return to heaven. They all feel like sojourners here on earth, and believe their real home is in the life beyond this one. And, they all believe they came back with a job to do.

"In the end," Dean says, "it was the prayers of the people who had gathered around me that summoned me back. If you were praying on that day, even though I was taken to heaven in the blink of an eye, your prayers would have beat me there. When a prayer is from the heart, it has no shelf life. There is no expiration date.

"I came to understand that it's very hard for a person you're praying for to go to hell. Of course, they make their own decision—but by your prayers, God Almighty is after them. Because of the prayers of my loved ones, I was sent back to tell this story."

Conclusion

WHICH ROAD WILL YOU CHOOSE?

As we finish our examination of the historical, sociological, religious, and biblical aspects of the afterlife, we are obliged once again to return to the questions that sparked our journey.

- Is there life after death?

- Is heaven real? And if so, how do you get there?

- Is hell real? And if so, how do you keep from going there?

Once again, as stated at the outset, no one can be talked into believing in the existence of an afterlife or the reality of heaven and hell. But earnest inquiry, a study of the facts with an open mind, can initiate the kind of reasonable and rational discourse, based on the Scriptures, that provides the answers we are seeking.

What we have found, by searching the historical accounts, studying the ethnographical evidence, and sincerely searching Scripture, is a compelling argument for the reality of life beyond the grave, and the belief that our eternal destination depends on how we live, act, and believe in this present life.

We've seen that, from the beginning of recorded history, every civilized culture has believed in an afterlife. Even primitive cultures of antiquity held strong beliefs in life beyond the grave. People seem to know instinctively that there must be more. It is part of the human psyche. I would even contend it is in our divine programming as created beings. Just as I believe we all have a void in our souls that can only be filled by a relationship with God, we all have a sense that we are here for a greater purpose and that there is more to life than this temporal realm.

Furthermore, most of these cultures have taught that the righteous dead go to a place of happiness and peace, while the unrighteous descend into a place of torment.

It seems incredible to me to think that so many cultures that never had contact with one another—that were separated in some cases by thousands of miles and thousands of years—should develop such similar ideas about what happens after we die. Although there are some differences in the specific details, the basic teaching about the existence of a paradise and a place of torment and punishment remains the same. It just makes sense to believe that there is at least a kernel of truth behind all of these various beliefs.

We've also seen that the Bible, both Old and New Testaments, has much to say about heaven and hell. You may have thought before you read this book that Judaism did not concern itself with the afterlife. As I've demonstrated, that is far from the truth. Heaven and hell are clearly present within the teachings of the Tanakh. And there is a great body of commentary about the afterlife—both heaven (Gan Eden, Olam Haba) and hell (Gehenna, Sheol, Hades) in the writings of the ancient Jewish sages. Once again, descriptions of the afterlife differ. But the basic idea remains the same: the righteous are ushered into paradise when their life on earth is over, while the wicked pass into a terrible place of punishment.

Furthermore, Jews as well as Christians have long believed in the resurrection of the dead at the end of the world, a time when the souls of the departed will be raised to new life. In fact, belief in the resurrection was at one time one of the hallmarks of the Jewish faith, and was even listed by Maimonides as one of his 13 principles of faith.

My intent, from the beginning, has been to show that ancient Jewish theology, as laid out in the sacred Hebrew texts and extra-biblical writings, has painted a clear and unequivocal picture of a destiny beyond the grave. God has used the Jewish people to reveal His plan and purpose for humankind through continuous revelation stretching back to the call of Abraham almost 4,000 years ago. Many Jewish people may have subsequently chosen to reject or renounce that revelation, but the voices of their own prophets and teachers speak loudly, even to us in today's supremely rationalistic world.

In the New Testament, we have an even clearer and more vivid presentation of a life beyond the grave. We are confronted by the teachings of Yeshua—Jesus of Nazareth—who tells us plainly that He came to show us the way to heaven:

> *Do not let your heart be troubled. Trust in God; trust also in Me. In My Father's house there are many dwelling places. If it were not so, would I have told you that I*

am going to prepare a place for you? If I go and prepare a place for you, I will come again and take you to Myself, so that where I am you may also be. And you know the way to where I am going (John 14:1-4).

He also asserted that He was *the only* way:

Thomas said to Him, "Master, we don't know where You are going. How can we know the way?" Yeshua said to him, "I am the way, the truth, and the life! No one comes to the Father except through Me" (John 14:5-6).

Jesus also said, "Amen, amen I tell you, if anyone keeps My word, he will never see death" (John 8:51). And, "I am the resurrection and the life! Whoever believes in Me, even if he dies, shall live. And whoever lives and believes in Me shall never die" (John 11:25-26).

And, of course, there are passages like John 3:16 and 1 John 5:12 (NIV):

For God so loved the world that He gave His one and only Son, that whoever believes in Him shall not perish but have eternal life.

Whoever has the Son has life; whoever does not have the Son of God does not have life.

These Scriptures are clear enough. They all convey that faith in Yeshua the Messiah is necessary to enter heaven. We must either accept or reject them. There is no middle ground.

I've also presented the astonishing accounts of a handful out of thousands, if not millions, who have lived through Near-Death Experiences and returned to tell about them. People like Howard

Storm, Dr. Gary Wood, Don Piper, Bill Wiese, and Earthquake Kelley. A common theme among their stories is that the biblical accounts of heaven and hell are true and accurate. Another common thread is the heartfelt yearning each of these men have to return as soon as possible to the paradise they experienced. That, in itself, is powerful evidence of the truth of their accounts.

Let me take just a moment to go back and touch upon what we have heard from these men:

Howard Storm

> When a person has a love of God and expresses that love in their life, they are attracted to God and He is attracted to them. It is literally like a magnet. The angels come and take those people to heaven where they become more perfect beings, enjoying eternity with God. People who don't like God and have rejected Him are repelled by Him. Although God doesn't want anybody to reject Him, and it is His desire that everyone find a home with Him, God doesn't make people go to hell. People who reject God get exactly their desire. And they get to go to a place where they're not going to be bothered by God anymore. They take every good thing that God gives us in this world for granted. But in hell, all the good things that God gives us are totally absent, because we have rejected them all, including the gift of life. Consequently, there is no goodness there, there's no beauty there. It has all been rejected. It's like a bunch of rats in a cage.

Dr. Gary L. Wood

Dying was the most peaceful and tranquil experience I ever had in my life. The first thing that happened was that I came straight out of my body. I was caught up in a massive, swirling, funnel-shaped cloud and bright, brilliant light. I saw my body lying over the steering wheel, but by that time, I was already caught up in heaven. It was the most serene experience I've ever had in my life—joyful, exuberant, happy. ...I came back with a message. Jesus told me to tell people never to buy in to the condemnation of the devil that they're unworthy. "Tell them they are worthy because I redeem them with My blood."

Don Piper

I was sent back with a message. The message is simple: heaven is real. It's a real place and God wants you to go there. But you're going to have to trust Jesus. He said, "I am the way, the truth, and the life. No one comes to the Father except through Me." Heaven is real and Jesus is the way. It's as simple as that.

Bill Wiese

When I met Jesus, He wept because He didn't want people to go to hell. It's way past our knowledge to understand how much He loves us. All we have to do is be humble enough to admit we're sinners, accept what Jesus has done in our behalf, and He'll save us.

Earthquake Kelley

Please hear me. Every moment of every day, people are dying lost and going to hell. What is more positive than wanting to keep people out of hell? I've been to hell. And I don't want anybody else to go there. ...I have been tormented, and I have heard the cries of those who are tormented and lost forever. If you spend eternity in hell, you constantly will be reminded of what a fool you were for listening to the devil's lies. You will replay every sermon you ever heard. You will remember every person who gave you an invitation to turn your life to Jesus. And you will spend eternity begging for another chance.

Dean Braxton

When I saw Him (Yeshua) for the first time all I could say was, "You did this for me?" I knew the only reason I was there (in heaven) was because of what He did for me, and for us all, on the cross. All I could do was repeat over and over, "Thank You, thank You, thank You!" Everything about me was praising Him. The first thing I praised Him for was when I saw how He was looking at me—as if I had never sinned in my life—like I never did anything wrong. Of course we know that when He forgives, He forgets. But it's one thing to have that knowledge and another to actually experience it personally. I was past just believing it: I was experiencing it, living it in the eternal moment.

Of course, in the end, the decision to believe or not is up to you. Jew or Christian, agnostic or atheist, we are all confronted with this fundamental choice. My fervent hope in writing this book has been to provide a clear and informed presentation of the proof that Scripture provides.

In summation, heaven is real, hell is real, and we are all destined to live on in eternity. Where you choose to spend that eternity is the most important decision you will ever make.

ENDNOTES

CHAPTER 1

1. Dinesh D'Souza, *Life After Death: The Evidence* (Washington, DC: Regnery Publishing, Inc., 2009), 7.

2. C.S. Lewis, *Mere Christianity* (New York: MacMillan, 1952), 19-20.

3. Ibid., 19.

4. Ibid., 22-23.

5. D'Souza, *Life After Death,* 139.

6. Ibid., 141-142.

7. Ibid., 143-44.

8. Francis Schaeffer, *How Shall We Then Live?* (Old Tappan, NJ: Fleming H. Revell Co., 1976), 224.

CHAPTER 2

1. N.T. Wright, *Surprised by Hope* (New York: Harper Collins, 2008), 11-12.

2. Owen Strachan and Douglas Sweeney, *Jonathan Edwards on Heaven & Hell* (Chicago: Moody Publishers, 2010), 36.

3. Terry Scott Taylor, "Skeptic's Song," 1976.

4. Raymond A. Moody, *The Light Beyond* (London: Rider & Company, 2005), 26-27.

5. Ibid., 151.

6. Maurice S. Rawlings, M.D., *To Hell and Back* (Nashville, TN: Thomas Nelson Publishers, 1993), 47-48.

7. Elizabeth L. Hillstrom, *Testing the Spirits* (Downer's Grove, IL: Intervarsity Press, 1995), 87.

8. Ibid., 88.

9. Ibid.

10. D'Souza, *Life After Death*, 66-67.

11. John F. MacArthur, *The Glory of Heaven* (Wheaton, IL: Crossway Publishers, 1996), 40-41.

12. Ibid., 41.

13. Rawlings, *To Hell and Back*, 61-62.

14. Ibid., 50.

CHAPTER 3

1. Americans Describe Their Views About Life After Death, Barna. org, October 21, 2003.

2. Pirke Avot 6:9.

3. Alfred J. Kolatch, *The Jewish Book of Why* (Middle Village, NY: Jonathan David Publishers, 1981), 52-53.

4. "Heaven—Where Is It? How Do We Get There?," ABCNews.com, December 20, 2005.

5. Dr. Reggie Anderson, *Appointments with Heaven* (Carol Stream, IL: Tyndale House Publishers, 2013), 278-280.

6. D'Souza, *Life After Death,* 74.

7. Ibid, 89.

8. Matthew 7:13-14.

CHAPTER 4

1. Jonathan Bernis, *A Rabbi Looks at Jesus of Nazareth* (Bloomington, MN: Chosen Books, 2010), 164-165.

2. Ibid., 169.

3. Flavius Josephus, *Antiquities*, B. 18, Ch. 1, ß3.

4. "Ancient Jewish History: Pharisees, Sadducees and Essenes"; Virtual Jewish Library.

5. Rifat Sonsino and Daniel B. Syme, *What Happens After I Die?* (New York: UAHC Press, 1990), 9.

6. Ibid., 7.

7. Albert Einstein Site Online, www.alberteinstein.com/quotes; accessed 8/26/14.

8. Sigmund Freud, *The Future of an Illusion* (New York: W.W. Norton, 1989), 42.

9. Abba Hillel Silver, *Where Judaism Differed: an inquiry into the distinctiveness of Judaism* (New York: MacMillan, 1956), 277.

10. Alan M. Dershowitz, *The Vanishing American Jews: In Search of Jewish Identity for the Next Century* (Boston: Little, Brown, 2000), 208.

11. Dennis Prager, "Jews and the Afterlife," *The Jewish Journal*, February 23, 2010.

12. Abraham Joshua Heschel, *Moral Grandeur and Spiritual Audacity* (New York: MacMillan, 1997), 411.

13. Ibid., 367.

14. Rabbi Yitz Greenberg, "Ask the Rabbis: Do Jews Believe in an Afterlife?" *Moment* magazine, July/August 2011.

15. Sonsino and Syme, *What Happens After I Die?*, 22.

16. Luke 16:19-31.

17. Enoch 66:8-10.

18. Sonsino and Syme, *What Happens After I Die?*, 38.

19. Pirkei Avos 4:21-22.

20. Moed Katan 9a.

21. Tanhuma Vayikra 8.

22. Immanuel ben Solomon of Rome, *Tophet and Eden (Hell and Paradise)* (London: University of London, 1921), 46.

23. Sonsino and Syme, *What Happens After I Die?*, 25.

24. Pesikta Rabbati 44:8.

25. Pesikta Rabbati 2:3.

26. Tosefta Sanhedrin 13:2.

27. Mishneh Torah Repentence 3:5.

28. Moses Maimonides, *Guide to the Perplexed 1:41*, translated by S. Pines (Chicago: University of Chicago Press, 1963), 91.

29. Babylonian Talmud, tractate Ketubot 111b.

30. Saadia ben Yosef al-Fayyumi, quoted in religion facts.com, Jewish Beliefs on the Afterlife.

31. Simcha Paull Raphael, *Jewish Views of the Afterlife* (Lanham, MD: Rowman and Littlefield Publishers, 2009), 119.

32. Sonsino and Syme, *What Happens After I Die?*, 136-140.

33. Ibid., 74-75.

34. Ibid., 56-58.

CHAPTER 5

1. First Epistle of Clement of Rome, Chapter 6.

2. "Fragments of the Lost Work of Justin on the Resurrection," www.earlychristianwritings.com.

3. Origen, *First Principles, Book II,* Chapter XI.6.

4. Jeffrey Burton Russell, *A History of Heaven: The Singing Silence* (Princeton, NJ: Princeton University Press, 1997), 55.

5. Colleen McDannell and Bernhard Lang, *Heaven: A History* (New Haven, CT: Yale University Press, 2001), 23.

6. Ibid., 32.

7. Chris Armstrong, "How the Early Church Saw Heaven," ChristianHistory.net.

8. Eusebius Bishop of Caesarea, extract from "Theophania," cited at www.christianforums.com.

9. Armstrong, "How the Early Church Saw Heaven," ChristianHistory.net.

10. McDannell and Lang, *Heaven: A History*, 47.

11. Ibid.

12. Billy Graham, *The Heaven Answer Book* (Nashville, TN: Thomas Nelson Publishers, 2012), 3, 130-131.

13. Derek Leman, *The World to Come: A Portal to Heaven on Earth* (Clarksville, MD: Lederer Books, 2008), 59.

14. Wayne Martindale, *Beyond the Shadowlands* (Wheaton, IL: Crossway Books, 2005), 47.

15. John F. MacArthur, *The Glory of Heaven* (Wheaton, IL: Crossway Books, 1996), 125, 134.

16. Martindale, *Beyond the Shadowlands,* 34.

17. Ibid.

18. Randy Alcorn, *Heaven* (Wheaton, IL: Tyndale House Publishers, 2004), Questions and Answers from pages 278, 332, 385, 305, 317, 319, 406-407.

CHAPTER 6

1. Lee Strobel, *The Case for Faith* (Grand Rapids, MI: Zondervan, 2000), 175.

2. Ibid., 193.

3. Wayne Martindale, *Beyond the Shadowlands* (Wheaton, IL: Crossway Books, 2005), 133.

4. C.S. Lewis, *The Great Divorce* (San Francisco, CA: Harper & Row, 1973), 39-40.

5. N.T. Wright, *For All the Saints* (Harrisburg, PA: Morehouse Publishing, 2004), 42.

6. Ibid., 43.

7. Brian Jones, *Hell Is Real (But I Hate to Admit It)* (Colorado Springs, CO: David C. Cook, 2011).

8. Ibid., 21.

9. Ibid., 23.

10. Ibid., 26-27.

CHAPTER 7

1. The Independent.com/Elisabeth Kübler Ross/Obituaries/News, August 28, 2004.

2. Berakot 57b.

3. P Sanhedrin 29b.

4. Simcha Paull Raphael, *Jewish Views of the Afterlife*, (Lanham, MD: Rowman and Littlefield Publishers, 2009), 142.

5. Erubin 19a.

6. Raphael, *Jewish Views of the Afterlife*, 98.

7. Sonsino and Syme, *What Happens After I Die?*, 27.

8. Ibid.

9. Raphael, *Jewish Views of the Afterlife*, 142, 145.

10. Shabbat 39b.

11. Raphael, *Jewish Views of the Afterlife*, 75.

12. Ibid., 176.

13. Ibid.

14. Ibid.

15. Ibid., 177.

16. Ibid., 178.

CHAPTER 8

1. Justin Martyr, *First Apology 12* [A.D. 151].

2. Theophilus of Antioch, *To Autolycus 1:14* [A.D. 181].

3. Hippolytus, *Against the Greeks* [A.D. 212].

4. Michael E. Wittmer, *Christ Alone* (Grand Rapids, MI: Edenridge Press, 2011), 137.

5. John F. Walvoord, Zachary J. Hayes, Clark H. Pinnock, *Four Views of Hell* (Grand Rapids, MI: Zondervan, 2010).

6. Christopher W. Morgan and Robert A. Peterson, *Hell Under Fire* (Grand Rapids, MI: Zondervan, 2004), 196.

7. Ibid., 12.

8. Ibid., 27.

9. Ibid., 32.

10. Ibid., 93.

11. Strachan and Sweeney, *Jonathan Edwards on Heaven & Hell,* 76-77.

12. Ibid.

13. Ibid., 142.

14. Ibid., 147.

CHAPTER 11

1. Dr. Gary L. Wood, *A Place Called Heaven* (Mustang, OK: Tate Publishing, 2008), 29.

CHAPTER 14

1. Bishop Earthquake Kelley, *Bound to Lose Destined to Win* (Cleveland, TN: CopperScoll Publishers, 2007), 59.

ABOUT THE AUTHOR

JONATHAN BERNIS HAS WORKED on the forefront of world evangelism since 1984, taking the Good News of Israel's Messiah to the far reaches of the earth, to the Jewish people, and also to the nations.

Today, as President of Jewish Voice Ministries International (JVMI) and associated organizations in Canada and the United Kingdom, Jonathan directs all aspects of the ministry, including the weekly television program *Jewish Voice with Jonathan Bernis*, which airs throughout the United States, Canada, Europe, Africa, and Asia.

JVMI's mission is two-fold: to proclaim the Gospel to the Jew first, and also to the nations (Romans 1:16), and to equip the Church—providing education about the Hebraic roots of Christianity, the Church's responsibility to Israel and the Jewish people, and how to share Messiah with the Jewish people. The Good News is proclaimed through television, print media, humanitarian/medical outreaches, and large-scale international festivals.

More than 561,390 people have attended JVMI's vibrant *Hear O' Israel! Festivals of Jewish Music & Dance* throughout Eastern Europe, India, and South America. Millions more have participated via television broadcasts. Thousands have responded to altar calls, and about one third of those who have responded have been Jewish. More than a dozen new Messianic Jewish congregations have been birthed in the former Soviet Union through these outreaches. JVMI also partners with several other Messianic ministries to establish and operate Messianic Jewish Bible Institutes around the world to train leaders for Jewish ministry.

The lost and scattered tribes of Israel are of particular interest to Jonathan and Jewish Voice. A prophetic sign of redemption, as God is revealing these enigmatic peoples from Ethiopia to Eastern India, Jewish Voice has mobilized to reach out with essential humanitarian and medical provision, as God's arm extended in the love of their Messiah. This is a very exciting and rewarding area of ministry, particularly close to Jonathan's heart as these are the poorest Jewish communities on the earth.

A sought-after speaker, Jonathan also teaches at seminars and conferences worldwide. He is a prominent leader in the Messianic movement and is a passionate supporter of Israel. He is the author of several books including, *A Rabbi Looks at Jesus of Nazareth* and *Confessing the Hebrew Scriptures: Adonai—Jehovah Rof•e•cha (The Lord Your Healer)*.

Jonathan is the founding Rabbi of Congregation Shema Yisrael in Rochester, New York, where he served as Senior Messianic Rabbi from 1984 to 1993. He also founded and pastored the Messianic Center of Saint Petersburg, Russia, where he lived and ministered from 1993 to 1997.

Jonathan and his wife, Elisangela, are the parents of two daughters, Liel and Hannah, and reside in Phoenix, Arizona.

"I am not ashamed of the gospel, because it is the power of God for the salvation of everyone who believes: first for the Jew, then for the Gentile" (Romans 1:16).

Jewish Voice Ministries International has a two-fold mission: to proclaim the Gospel to the Jew first, and also to the Nations (Romans 1:16), and to equip the Church by providing education about the Hebraic roots of Christianity, the Church's responsibility to Israel and the Jewish People, and how to share Messiah with the Jewish People.

The Good News is proclaimed through television, print and online media, international festival outreaches, medical clinics/humanitarian aid to the Lost Tribes of Israel scattered throughout Africa and India, and in planting and strengthening congregations to disciple new believers who come to faith in Jesus.

Find out more about Jewish Voice at www.jewishvoice.org or 1-800-299-9374.